Introduction
to advanced study in music education

Introduction to advanced study

Neal E. Glenn
University of Iowa

Edgar M. Turrentine
University of Minnesota

in music education

WM. C. BROWN COMPANY PUBLISHERS DUBUQUE, IOWA

Printed in U. S. A.

Introduction

It has long been a truism that this is an ever changing world. Nothing remains static. The world's knowledge is doubling and redoubling at an almost alarming rate. There was a time when the educational process was thought to be a terminal process, but that viewpoint receives very little consideration now. Rather, the educational process is considered as a continuing process. One needs only to examine his own living habits to confirm this. One is constantly acquiring new knowledge just to carry on his own day-to-day activities.

Consistent with this change, the patterns of formal education have been changing at a rapid rate and will continue to do so even more rapidly. There was a time, in the not too distant past, when one considered himself prepared for a lifetime of teaching after four years of collegiate instruction. Not so, now. Four years of collegiate instruction for the prospective teacher merely prepares him to start teaching. If he continues as a teacher, he also must continue as a student.

It is to this concept of *teacher-student,* that this book is addressed. It is hoped that it will serve, as its title suggests, as an introduction to further study for the music teacher just entering the profession. Its use is not necessarily restricted to those continuing their formal study, but also is extended to those continuing to study in an informal way. The contents have been so organized, hopefully, that the reader will gain an increased understanding of the historical and philosophical foundations of music teaching, an increased understanding of the contributions which research has and can contribute to music teaching, and an increased understanding of the skills demanded in solving problems related to music teaching.

PART I reflects the viewpoint that one's beliefs reflect one's actions. The commonality of beliefs begets a commonality of actions. Being able to identify the source of one's actions enables him to act more consistently and confidently. Therefore, the selected "readings" of PART I are presented as a means of becoming acquainted with and identifying several significant beliefs about music and music teaching which have had a more-than-passing influence on the actions of music and music teaching. To know what has gone before should enable one to cope with the present and, to a degree, to govern the future more consistently and confidently. It is hoped that these brief excerpts from the writings of these important contributors to education will send the reader on to their complete writings and to the writings of others.

When one is considering any single aspect of human behavior he must consider many different factors governing that behavior. This holds true for music as an aspect of human behavior. PART II concerns itself with several factors governing music and music teaching. Obviously, the authors have not discussed these factors comprehensively. These discussions merely serve, the authors hope, to whet the curiosity of the reader to delve more deeply into each of these factors, and to delve into other affective factors. A small number of related research studies have been summarized, and it is hoped the reader will refer to the original studies for more detailed analysis. It is also hoped the reader will be encouraged to conduct research projects of his own, formally or informally, in these and other factors concerning music and music teaching.

It has been said that research is a way of life. Most certainly every teacher, at some time or another, must do research, that is, solve problems in an orderly and knowledgeable manner. Especially do *teacher-students* often feel the necessity. As in every other productive effort, there are certain patterns and guidelines to problem-solving. One may solve a problem using a haphazard manner, but he will solve that problem more efficiently and effectively if he proceeds in a step-by-step manner. PART III attempts to help the reader establish an order to his problem-solving actions. The authors make no pretense that their suggestions are the only ways of conducting research, but they have been and can be effective. Probably the most important suggestion, which is largely implied, is that, for effective problem-solving, consistency and orderliness of action is paramount.

Brevity has been the criterion in the writing of this book. Verbosity is an enemy of introductions, and, in this instance, the authors believe there is nothing more discouraging to the eager and enthusiastic student than introductions to advanced study, research technique manuals, and other like tomes, whose distinguishing feature is length. This, the authors hope, possesses brevity and, the authors also hope, will serve as a practical and serviceable guide to continued study for those dedicated, alert, curious, and adventuresome music teachers who are about to, or who have just entered the profession.

Contents

PART II — RESEARCH

PART III — RESEARCH TECHNIQUES

POSTSCRIPT

Part I

READINGS

Excerpt, *The Republic*

Plato, the Greek philosopher, was born in 428 or 427 B.C. and died in 348 or 347 B.C. His influence on philosophical thought is immeasurable. Around 387 B.C. he founded his famous Academy, dedicated to the scientific and philosophic search for truth. Plato, undoubtedly an acquaintance of Socrates, based his moral philosophy on the Socratic doctrine that man's great purpose was to develop a moral, rational personality. The following reading is taken from Plato's *Republic*, one of his most significant dialogues. In the *Republic*, Plato is concerned with three main "arguments": the ethical and political, the aesthetic, and the metaphysical.

"But we must look for those craftsmen who by the happy gift of nature are capable of following the trail of true beauty and grace, that our young men, dwelling as it were in a salubrious region, may receive benefit from all things about them, whence the influence that emanates from works of beauty may waft itself to eye or ear like a breeze that brings from wholesome places health, and so from earliest childhood insensibly guide them to likeness, to friendship, to harmony with beautiful reason." "Yes," he said, "That would be far the best education for them." "And is it not for this reason, Glaucon," said I, "that education in music is most sovereign, because more than anything else rhythm and harmony find their way to the inmost soul and take strongest hold upon it, bringing with them and imparting grace, if one is rightly trained, and otherwise the contrary? And further, because omissions and the failure of beauty in things badly made or grown would be most quickly perceived by one who was properly educated in music, and so, feeling distaste rightly, he would praise beautiful things and take delight in them and receive them into his soul to foster its growth and become himself beautiful and good. The ugly he would rightly disapprove of and hate while still young and yet unable to apprehend the reason, but when reason came the man thus nurtured would be the first to give her welcome, for by this affinity he would know her." "I certainly think," he said, "that such is the cause of education in music." "It is, then," said I, "as it was when we learned our letters and felt that we knew them sufficiently only when the separate letters did not elude us, appearing as few elements in all the combinations that convey them, and when we did not disregard them in small things or great and think it unnecessary to recognize them, but were eager to distinguish them everywhere, in the belief that we should never be literate and letter-perfect till we could do this." "True." "And is it not also true that if there are any likenesses of letters reflected in water or mirrors, we shall never know them until we know the originals, but such knowledge belongs to the same art and discipline?" "By all means." "Then, by heaven, am I not right in saying that by the same token we shall never be true musicians, either — neither we, nor the guardians that we have undertaken to educate — until we are able to recognize the forms of soberness, courage, liberality, and high-mindedness and all their kindred and their opposites, too, in all the combinations that contain and convey them, and to apprehend them and their images wherever found, disregarding them neither in trifles nor in great things, but believing the knowlege of them to belong to the same art and discipline?" "The conclusion is inevitable," he said. "Then," said I, "when there is a coincidence of a beautiful disposition in the soul and corresponding and hamonious beauties of the same type in the bodily form — is not this the fairest spectacle for one who is capable of its contemplation?" "Far the fairest." "And surely the fairest is the most lovable." "Of course." "The true musician, then would love by preference persons of this sort; but if there were disharmony he would not love this." "No," he said, "not if there was a defect in the soul; but if it were in the body he would bear with it and still be willing to bestow his love." "I understand," I said, "that you have or have had favorites of this sort and I grant your distinction. But tell me this — can there be any communion between soberness and extravagant pleasure?" "How could there be," he said, "since such pleasure puts a man beside himself no less than pain?" "Or between it and virtue generally?" "By no means." "But is there between pleasure and insolence and license?" "Most assuredly." "Do you know of greater or keener pleasure than that associated with Aphrodite?" "I don't" he said, "nor yet of any more insane." "But is not the right love a sober and harmonious love of the orderly and the beautiful?" "It is indeed," said he. "Then nothing of madness, nothing akin to license, must be allowed to come nigh the right love." "No, by heaven, Socrates," he said, "it must not come nigh, nor may lover and beloved who rightly love and are loved have anything to do with it?" "Thus, then, as it seems, you will lay down the law in the city that we are founding, that the lover may kiss and pass the time with and touch the beloved as a father would a son, for honorable ends, if he persuade him. But otherwise he must so associate with the objects of his care that there should never be any suspicion of anything further, on penalty of being stigmatized for want of taste and true musical culture." "Even so," he said. "Do you not agree, then that our discourse on music has come to an end? It has certainly made a fitting end, for surely the end and consumation of culture is the love of the beautiful." "I concur," he said. . . .

. . . "For these two, then, it seems there are two arts which I would say some god gave to mankind, music and gymnastics for the service of the high-spirited principle and the love of knowledge in them — not for the soul and the body except incidentally, but for the harmonious adjustment of these two principles by the proper degree of tension and relaxation of each." "Yes, so it appears," he said. "Then he who best blends gymnastics with music and applies them most suitably to the soul is the man whom we should most rightly pronounce to be the most perfect and harmonious musician, far rather than the one who brings the strings into unison with one another." "That seems likely, Socrates," he said. "And shall we not also need in our city, Glaucon, a permanent overseer of this kind if its constitution is to be preserved?" "We most certainly shall."[1]

[1]Plato, *The Republic*, translated by Paul Shorey, The Loeb Classical Library (Cambridge: Harvard University Press, 1930-35), pp. 257-65 and 293-5. Reprinted by permission of the publishers and The Loeb Classical Library.

Excerpt, *Politics*

Aristotle, another influential Greek philosopher,
was born in 384 B.C. and died in 322 B.C. Early in
his life, at the age of seventeen, he was in attend-
ance at Plato's Academy and remained until Plato's
death. After a period away from Athens, during
which time he tutored Alexander, he returned and
established his own school, the Peripatetic, in the
Lyceum. His view of education was a three-fold
one: the education of the body, the education of
the desires and passions, and the education of the
reason. His development of the mode of reasoning,
called deductive, has influenced all scientific research since his time.

. . . our first inquiry is whether music ought not or ought to be included in education, and what is its efficacy among the three uses of
it that have been discussed — does it serve for education or amusement
or entertainment? It is reasonable to reckon it under all of these heads,
and it appears to participate in them all. Amusement is for the sake of
relaxation, and relaxation must necessarily be pleasant, for it is a way
of curing the pain due to laborious work; also entertainment ought
admittedly to be not only honorable but also pleasant, for happiness is
derived from both honor and pleasure; but we all pronounce music to
be one of the pleasantest things, whether instrumental or instrumental
and vocal music together (at least Musaeus says, "Song is man's sweetest
joy," and that is why people with good reason introduce it at parties
and entertainments, for its exhilarating effect), so that for this reason

also one might suppose that the younger men ought to be educated in music. For all harmless pleasures are not only suitable for the ultimate object but also for relaxation; and as it but rarely happens for men to reach their ultimate object, whereas they often relax and pursue amusement not so much with some ulterior object but because of the pleasure in it, it would be serviceable to let them relax at intervals in the pleasures derived from music. But it has come about that men make amusements an end; for the end also perhaps contains a certain pleasure, but not any ordinary pleasure, and seeking this they take the other as being this because it has a certain resemblance to the achievement of the end of their undertakings. For the end is desirable not for the sake of some future result, but because of things that have happened already, for instance labor and pain. One might then perhaps assume this to be the reason which causes men to seek to procure happiness by means of those pleasures; but in the case of taking part in music is useful, as it seems, for relaxation. But nevertheless we must examine whether it is not the case that, although this has come about, yet the nature of music is more honorable than corresponds with the employment of it mentioned, and it is proper not only to participate in the common pleasure that springs from it, which is perceptible to everybody (for the pleasure contained in music is of a natural kind, owing to which the use of it is dear to those of all ages and characters), but to see if its influence reaches also in a manner to the character and to the soul. And this would clearly be the case if we are affected in our characters in a certain manner by it. But it is clear that we are affected in a certain manner, both by many other kinds of music and not least by the melodies of Olympus; for these admittedly make our souls enthusiastic, and enthusiasm is an affection of the character of the soul. And moreover everybody when listening to imitations is thrown into a corresponding state of feelings, even apart from the rhythms and melodies themselves. And since it is the case that music is one of the things that give pleasure, and that virtue has to do with feeling delight and love and hatred rightly, there is obviously nothing that is more needful to learn and become habituated to than to judge correctly and to delight in virtuous characters and noble actions; but rhythms and melodies contain representations of anger and mildness, and also of courage and temperance and all their opposites and the other moral qualities, that most closely correspond to the true natures of these qualities (and this is clear from the facts of what occurs — when we listen to such representations we change in our soul); and habituation in feeling pain and delight at representations of reality is close to feeling them towards actual reality (for example, if a man delights in beholding the statue of somebody for no other reason than because of its actual form, the actual sight of the person whose statue he beholds must also of necessity give him pleasure); and it is the case that whereas the other objects of sensation contain no representation of character, for example the objects of touch and taste (though the objects of sight do so slightly, for there are forms that represent character, but only to a small extent, and not all men participate in visual perception of such qualities; also visual works of art are not representations of character but rather the forms and colors produced are mere indications of character, and these indications are only bodily sensations during the emotions; not but what in so far as there is a difference even in regard to the observation of these indications, the young must not look at the works of Pauson, but those of Polygnotus and of any other moral painter or sculptor), pieces of music on the contrary do actually contain in themselves imitations of character; and this is manifest, for even in the nature of the mere harmonies there are differences, so that people when hearing them are affected differently and have not the same feelings in regard to each of them, but listen to some in a more mournful and restrained state, for instance the harmony called Mixolydian, and to others in a softer state of mind, for instance the relaxed harmonies, but in a midway state and with the greatest composure to another, as the Dorian alone of harmonies seems to act, while the Phrygian makes men enthusiastic; for these things are well stated by those who have studied this form of education, as they derive the evidence for their theories from the actual facts of experience. And the same holds good about the rhythms also, for some have a more stable and others a more emotional character, and of the latter some are more vulgar in their emotional effects and others more liberal. From these considerations therefore it is plain that music has the power of producing a certain effect on the moral character of the soul, and if it has the power to do this, it is clear that the young must be directed to music and must be educated in it. Also education in music is well adapted to the youthful nature; for the young owing to their youth cannot endure anything not sweetened by pleasure, and music is by nature a thing that has a pleasant sweetness. And we seem to have a certain affinity with harmonies and rhythms; owing to which many wise men say either that the soul is a harmony or that it has harmony. . . .[2]

[2]Aristotle, *Politics*, translated by H. Rackham, The Loeb Classical Library (Cambridge: Harvard University Press, 1935), pp. 649-653. Reprinted by permission of the publishers and The Loeb Classical Library.

X.xxxiii, *Confessions*

Saint Augustine, born in Africa in A.D. 354 and, after a sojourn in what is now modern Italy, died in Africa in A.D. 430, after having served as Bishop of Hippo for a period of thirty-four years. Although the chronology of the *Confessions* may not be correct, this work does reveal the inner man. The following reading gives the reader an insight into the use of music and its effect upon the listener at this time in early Christian history.

The delights of mine ears, verily, have heretofore more strongly inveigled and engaged me; but thou hast brought me off and freed me. Yet still at hearing of those airs which thy words breathe soul into, whenas they are sung with a well tuned and well governed voice, I do, I confess, receive a little contentment; not so great though as that I am enchanted by it, but that I can go away when I please. But yet for all this, that those airs may together with these words (by virtue of which they receive life) gain full admission with me, do they aspire to be entertained into a place of no mean honour in this heart of mine, nor can I scarce afford them a room befitting for them. For sometimes forsooth, do I seem to myself to attribute more respect unto them than is seemly; yea, even whilst together with those sacred ditties I perceive our minds to be far more religiously and zealously blown up into a flame of devotion, whenas ditties are thus sung, than they would have been, had they not been so sung: yea, and I perceive withal, how that the several affections of our spirit, have their proper moods answerable to their variety in the voice and singing, and by some secret association therewith they be stirred up. But this contentment of my flesh (unto which it is not fit to give over the mind to be enervated) doth very often beguile me: the sense going not so along with the reason, as patiently to come behind it; but having for reason's sake gained admission, it strives even to run before and be her leader. Thus in these things I sometimes sin at unawares, but afterwards am aware of it.

Again at another time, through an indiscreet weariness of being inveigled, do I err out of too precise a severity: yea, very fierce am I sometimes, in the desire of having the melody of all pleasant music, to which David's Psalter is so often sung, banished both from mine own ears, and out of the whole church too: and the safer way it seems unto me, which I remember to have been often told me of Athanasius, Bishop of Alexandria, who caused the reader of the psalm to sound it forth with so little warbling of the voice, as that it was nearer to speaking, than to singing. Notwithstanding, so often as I call to mind the tears I shed at the hearing of thy church songs, in the beginning of my recovered faith, yea, and at this very time, whenas I am moved not with the singing, but with the thing sung (when namely they are set off with a clear voice and suitable modulation), I then acknowledge the great good use of this institution. Thus float I between peril of pleasure, and an approved profitable custom: inclined the more (though herein I pronounce no irrevocable opinion) to allow of the old usage of singing in the Church; that so by the delight taken in at the ears, the weaker minds be roused up into some feeling of devotion. And yet again, so oft as it befalls me to be more moved with the voice than with the ditty, I confess myself to have grievously offended: at which time I wish rather not to have heard the music. See now in what a state I am! Weep with me, and weep for me, O all you, who inwardly feel any thoughts, whence good actions do proceed. As for you that feel none such, these things move not you. But thou, O Lord my God, look upon me, hearken, and behold, and pity, and heal me, thou in whose eyes I am now become a problem to myself; and that is my infirmity.[3]

[3]St. Augustine, *Confessions*, translated by William Watts, The Loeb Classical Library (New York: G. P. Putnam's Sons, 1912), pp. 165-9. Reprinted by permission of the publishers and The Loeb Classical Library.

Preface to George Rhau's
Symphoniae incundae, 1538

Martin Luther, the son of a miner, was born on November 10, 1483, at Eisleben and died in the same village on February 18, 1546. After gaining a Master's degree at the University of Erfurt, he began the study of law, but after two months of study he entered the monastery of the Augustinian Eremites in Erfurt and was ordained a priest in 1507. With the posting of his 95 theses on the door of the Castle church at Wittenberg on October 31, 1517, he embarked on his well-known career as religious reformer. Luther was a very musical man, indeed, his musical activities supported him in his early education and, in later life, his hymn writing and concern for music earned him a prominent place in music history. His concern with education was great, and he encouraged each town and village to set up and maintain its own school and to teach music, among other subjects, in the school.

Greetings in Christ! I would certainly like to praise music with all my heart as the excellent gift of God which it is and to commend it to everyone. But I am so overwhelmed by the diversity and magnitude of its virtue and benefits that I can find neither beginning nor end or method for my discourse. As much as I want to commend it, my praise is bound to be wanting and inadequate. For who can comprehend it all? And even if you wanted to encompass all of it, you would appear to have grasped nothing at all. First then, looking at music itself, you will find that from the beginning of the world it has been instilled and implanted in all creatures, individually and collectively. For nothing is without sound or harmony. Even the air, which of itself is invisible and imperceptible to all our senses, and which, since it lacks both voice and speech, is the least musical of all things, becomes sonorous, audible, and comprehensible when it is set in motion. Wondrous mysteries are here suggested by the Spirit, but this is not the place to dwell on them. Music is still more wonderful in living things, especially birds, so that David, the most musical of all the kings and minstrel of God, in deepest wonder and spiritual exultation praised the astounding art and ease of the song of birds when he said in Psalm 104, "By them the birds of the heaven have their habitation; they sing among the branches."

And yet, compared to the human voice, all this hardly deserves the name of music, so abundant and incomprehensible is here the munificence and wisdom of our most gracious Creator. Philosophers have labored to explain the marvelous instrument of the human voice: how can the air projected by a light movement of the tongue and an even lighter movement of the throat produce such an infinite variety and articulation of the voice and of words? And how can the voice, at the direction of the will, sound forth so powerfully and vehemently that it cannot only be heard by everyone over a wide area, but also be understood? Philosophers for all their labor cannot find the explanation; and baffled they end in perplexity; for none of them has yet been able to define or demonstrate the original components of the human voice, its sibilation and (as it were) its alphabet, e.g., in the case of laughter — to say nothing of weeping. They marvel, but they do not understand. But such speculations on the infinite wisdom of God, shown in this single part of his creation, we shall leave to better men with more time on their hands. We have hardly touched on them.

Here it must suffice to discuss the benefit of this great art. But even that transcends the greatest eloquence of the most eloquent, because of the infinite variety of its forms and benefits. We can mention only one point (which experience confirms), namely, that next to the Word of God, music deserves the highest praise. She is a mistress and governess of those human emotions — to pass over the animals — which as masters govern men or more often overwhelm them. No greater commendation than this can be found — at least not by us. For whether you wish to comfort the sad, to terrify the happy, to encourage the despairing, to humble the proud, to calm the passionate, or to appease those full of hate — and who could number all these masters of the human heart, namely, the emotions, inclinations, and affections that impel men to evil or good? — what more effective means than music could you find? The Holy Ghost himself honors her as an instrument for his proper work when in his Holy Scriptures he asserts that through her his gifts were instilled in the prophets, namely, the inclination to all virtues, as can be seen in Elisha. On the other hand, she serves to cast out Satan, the instigator of all sins, as is shown in Saul, the king of Israel.

Thus it was not without reason that the fathers and prophets wanted nothing else to be associated as closely with the Word of God as music. Therefore, we have so many hymns and Psalms where message and music join to move the listener's soul, while in other living beings and bodies music remains a language without words. After all, the gift of language combined with the gift of song was only given to man to let him know that he should praise God with both word and music, namely, by proclaiming through music and by providing sweet melodies with words. For even a comparison between different men will show how rich and manifold our glorious Creator proves himself in distributing the gifts of music, how much men differ from each other in voice and manner of speaking so that one amazingly excels the other. No two men can be found with exactly the same voice and manner of speaking, although they often seem to imitate each other, the one as it were being the ape of the other.

But when (musical) learning is added to all this and artistic music which corrects, develops, and refines the natural music, then at last it is possible to taste with wonder (yet not to comprehend) God's absolute and perfect wisdom in his wondrous work of music. Here it is most remarkable that one single voice continues to sing the tenor, while at the same time many other voices play around it, exulting and adorning it in exuberant strains and, as it were, leading it forth in a divine roundelay, so that those who are the least bit moved know nothing more amazing in this world. But any who remain unaffected are unmusical indeed and deserve to hear a certain filth poet or the music of the pigs.

But the subject is much too great for me briefly to describe all its benefits. And you, my young friend, let this noble, wholesome, and cheerful creation of God be commended to you. By it you may escape shameful desires and bad company. At the same time you may by this creation accustom yourself to recognize and praise the Creator. Take special care to shun perverted minds who prostitute this lovely gift of nature and of art with their erotic rantings; and be quite assured that none but the devil goads them on to defy their very nature which would and should praise God its Maker with this gift, so that these Bastards purloin the gift of God and use it to worship the foe of God, the enemy of nature and of this lovely art. Farewell in the Lord.[4]

---

[4]Ulrich S. Leupold, editor. *Liturgy and Hymns*, Vol. 53 of *Luther's Works*, Helmut T. Lehmann, general editor. (Philadelphia: Fortress Press, 1965), pp. 321-4. Reprinted by permission of the publishers.

"The Method of the Arts,"
The Great Didactic

Johann Comenius was born in 1592 and died in 1670. He was the last of the Moravian-Bohemian clergy to hold the office of presiding bishop of the Moravian church. He is remembered as an educational reformer. Besides his many writings, he was asked to reform the Swedish schools but was unable to complete the task because of his differing religious views. It has been hinted that he may have been asked to become the first president of Harvard University. Comenius advocated a universal education.

1. "Theory," says Vives, "is easy and short, but has no result other than the gratification that it affords. Practice, on the other hand, is difficult and prolix, but is of immense utility." Since this is so, we should diligently seek out a method by which the young may be easily led to the practical application of natural forces, which is to be found in the arts.

2. Art primarily requires three things: (1) A model or a conception; that is to say, an external form which the artist may examine and then try to imitate. (2) The material on which the new form is to be impressed. (3) The instruments by the aid of which the work is accomplished.

3. But when the instruments, the materials, and the model have been provided, three more things are necessary before we can learn an art: (1) a proper use of the materials; (2) skilled guidance; (3) frequent practice. That is to say, the pupil should be taught when and

15

how to use his materials; he should be given assistance when using them that he may not make mistakes, or that he may be corrected if he do; and he should not leave off making mistakes and being corrected until he can work correctly and quickly.

4. With respect to these points eleven canons must be observed: six on the use of materials; three on guidance; and two on practice.

5. (i) What has to be done must be learned by practice. . . . In schools, therefore, let the students learn to write by writing, to talk by talking, to sing by singing, and to reason by reasoning. . . .

6. (ii) A definite model of that which has to be made must always be provided.

This the student should first examine, and then imitate, as though he were following in the footsteps of a guide. For he who neither knows what has to be done nor how to do it, is unable to produce anything of himself, but must have a model placed before him. Indeed it is sheer cruelty to force any one to do what you wish, while he is ignorant what your wishes are; . . .

7. (iii) The use of instruments should be shown in practice and not by words; that is to say, by example rather than by precept.

. . . No one has ever mastered any language or art by precept alone; while by practice this is possible, even without precept.

8. (iv) Practice should commence with the rudiments and not with ambitious works.

9. (v) Beginners should at first practice on a material that is familiar to them.

. . . Its meaning is that students should not be overburdened with matters that are unsuitable to their age, comprehension, and present condition, since otherwise they will spend their time in wrestling with shadows. . . .

10. (vi) At first the precribed form should be imitated with exactness. Later on more freedom may be allowed.

11. (vii) The models of the objects that have to be produced must be as perfect as is possible, so that if any one exercise himself sufficiently in imitating them it will be possible for him to become perfect in his art.

12. (viii) The first attempt at imitation should be as accurate as possible, that not the smallest deviation from the model be made.

That is to say, as far as is possible. For whatever comes first is, as it were, the foundation of that which follows. . . . Timotheus the musician used to demand twice as large a fee from those pupils who had learned the rudiments of their art elsewhere, saying that his labour was twofold, as he had first to get them out of the bad habits that they had acquired, and then to teach them correctly. Those, therefore, who are learning any art should take care to make themselves masters of the rudiments by imitating their copies accurately. . . . a delay which is caused by obtaining a thorough grip of first principles is really no delay, but an advance towards mastering what follows with ease, speed, and accuracy.

13. (ix) Errors must be corrected by the master on the spot; but precepts, that is to say the rules, and the exceptions to the rules, must be given at the same time.

Hitherto we have urged that the arts be taught rather by example than by precept: we now add that precepts and rules must be given as well, that they may guide the operations and prevent error. . . . Reasons should also be given for each rule. In this way a thorough knowledge of the art, and confidence and exactness in imitating, will be attained.

14. (x) The perfect teaching of art is based on synthesis and analysis.

15. For all this, the accurate analysis of the work of others must not be neglected. . . . Many processes require many rules to express them, and these we can only learn if we analyse and study, and by imitation and emulation put ourselves in a position to produce similar results.

16. It is our wish then that in each art complete and exact models or examples of everything that can be produced in that art be supplied to the student. Precepts also and rules should be given him to help him to carry out the processes, to guide his efforts at imitation, to show him how to avoid making faults, and to correct them when made. Then other and different models should be given him, and these he should learn to classify and compare with the models that he has already used, and by copying a model that is like one previously used to produce work that resembles the original. After this, the finished works of other artists (who must be well known) may be examined and analysed in accordance with the models and rules that are already familiar. In this way the student will learn to employ the rules with greater ease, and will acquire the art of concealing his art. Only after a course of exercises of this kind will he be in the position to criticise artistic productions, whether his own or those of others.

17. (xi) These exercises must be continued until artistic production becomes second nature.

For it is practice, and nothing else, that produces an artist.[5]

---

[5]Johann Comenius, *The Great Didactic,* translated by M. W. Keatinge. (London: A. & C. Black, Ltd. 1907), Part II, pp. 194-202.

"Musick," *Some Thoughts Concerning Education*

∽∾∿∾∿∾∿∾∿∾∿

John Locke, champion of religious toleration and civil liberty, was born on August 29, 1632, Wrington, Somersetshire, England. Locke, the philosopher, is best known for his "sense perception" philosophy. His educational philosophy was that education should build "character." The child, he believed, should be taught "useful" subjects. "Recreational" subjects should be taught, also, but not too much time spent on them. Locke died on October 28, 1704.

197. *Musick* is thought to have some Affinity with Dancing, and a good Hand upon some Instruments is by many People mightily valued. But it wastes so much of a young Man's Time to gain but a moderate Skill in it; and engages often in such odd Company, that many think it much better spared: And I have amongst Men of Parts and Business so seldom heard any one commended or esteemed for having an Excellency in *Musick,* that amongst all those things that ever came into the List of Accomplishments, I think I may give it the last Place. Our short Lives will not serve us for the Attainment of all Things; nor can our Minds be always intent on something to be learned. The Weakness of our Constitutions both of Mind and Body, requires that we should be often unbent: And he that will make a good use of any Part of his Life, must allow a large Portion of it to Recreation. At least, this must not be denied to young People; unless whilst you with too much Haste make them old, you have the Displeasure to set them in their Graves or a second Childhood sooner than you could wish. And therefore, I

think, that the Time and Pains allotted to serious Improvements, should be employed about things of most Use and Consequence, and that too in the Methods the most easy and short that could be at any rate obtained: And perhaps, as I have above said, it would be none of the least Secrets of Education, to make the Exercises of the Body and the Mind the *Recreation* one to another. I doubt not but that something might be done in it, by a prudent Man, that would well consider the Temper and Inclination of his Pupil. For he that is wearied either with Study or Dancing does not desire presently to go to sleep, but to do something else which may divert and delight him. But this must be always remembered, that nothing can come into the Account of *Recreation*, that is not done with Delight.[6]

---

[6]John Locke, *Some Thoughts Concerning Education*, R. H. Quick, editor. (Cambridge: Harvard University Press, 1902), pp. 174-5.

"Letter XXII: Training of Eye and Ear -- Music Education,"

Letters to Greaves

∽∾∿∾∿∾∿∾∿

Johann Pestalozzi was born in Zurich on January 12, 1746, and died on February 17, 1827. He is remembered for his great concern for the poor and their children, but is far better remembered as a great educational reformer. In 1805, at Yverdon, he founded his famous school, based on "sense impression." One knows only because one has observed actual objects and experienced concrete things. Important, too, at Yverdon was the teacher-training division he set up to train teachers in his educational beliefs. His influence was spread throughout the United States by the Oswego Normal School.

It will be well to connect these exercises very early with others, tending to form the taste. It seems not to be sufficiently understood that good taste and good feelings are kindred to each other, and that they reciprocally confirm each other. Though the ancients have said that "to study those arts which are suited to a free-born mind soothes the character, and takes away the roughness of exterior manners," yet little has been done to give free access to those enjoyments or accomplishments to all, or even to the majority of the people. If it is not possible for them to give much of their attention to subordinate or ornamental pursuits, while so much of their time is taken up by providing for their first and necessary wants, still, this does not furnish a conclusive reason why they should be shut out altogether from every pursuit above the toil of their ordinary avocations.

Now that I am on the topic, I will not let the opportunity pass by without speaking of one of the most effective aids of moral education. You are aware that I mean *Music*; and you are not only acquainted with my sentiments on that subject, but you have also observed the very satisfactory results which we have obtained in our schools. The exertions of my excellent friend Nageli, who has with equal taste and judgment reduced the highest principles of his art to the simplest elements, have enabled us to bring our children to a proficiency which, on any other plan, must be the work of much time and labour.

But it is not the proficiency which I would describe as a desirable accomplishment in education. It is the marked and most beneficial influence of music on the feelings, which I have always thought and always observed to be most efficient in preparing or attuning, as it were, the mind for the best of impressions. The exquisite harmony of a superior performance, the studied elegance of the execution, may indeed give satisfaction to a connoisseur; but it is the simple and untaught grace of melody which speaks to the heart of every human being. Our own national melodies, which have since time immemorial been resounding in our native valleys, are fraught with reminiscences of the brightest page of our history, and of the most endearing scenes of domestic life. But the effect of music in education is not only to keep alive a national feeling: it goes much deeper; if cultivated in the right spirit, it strikes at the root of every bad or narrow feeling: of every ungenerous or mean prosperity, of every emotion unworthy of humanity. In saying so I might quote an authority which commands our attention on account of the elevated character and genius of the man from whom it proceeds. It is well known that there was not a more eloquent and warm advocate of the moral virtues of music than the venerable Luther. But though his voice has made itself heard, and is still held in the highest esteem among us, yet experience has spoken still louder, and more unquestionably, to the truth of the proposition which he was among the first to vindicate. Experience has long since proved that a system proceeding upon the principle of sympathy would be imperfect, if it were to deny itself the assistance of that powerful means of the culture of the heart. Those schools, or those families in which music has retained the cheerful and chaste character which it is so important that it should preserve have invariably displayed scenes of moral feeling, and consequently of happiness, which leave no doubt as to the intrinsic value of that art, which has sunk in neglect, or degenerated into abuse, only in the ages of barbarism or depravity.

I need not remind you of the importance of music in engendering and assisting the highest feelings of which man is capable. It is almost universally acknowledged that Luther has seen the truth, when he pointed out music, devoid of studied pomp and vain ornament, in its solemn and impressive simplicity, as one of the most efficient means of elevating and purifying genuine feelings of devotion.

We have frequently, in our conversations on this subject, been at a loss how to account for the circumstance that in your own country, though that fact is as generally acknowledged, yet music does not form a more prominent feature in general education. It would seem that the notion prevails, that it would require more time and application than can conveniently be bestowed upon it to make its influence extend also on the education of the people.

Now I would appeal, with the same confidence as I would to yourself, to any traveller, whether he has not been struck with the facility, as well as the success, with which it is cultivated among us. Indeed, there is scarcely a village school throughout Switzerland, and perhaps there is none throughout Germany or Prussia, in which something is not done for an acquirement at least of the elements of music on the new and more appropriate plan. This is a fact which it cannot be difficult to examine, and which it will be impossible to dispute; and I will conclude this letter by expressing the hope which we have been entertaining together, that this fact will not be overlooked in a country which has never been backward in suggesting or adopting improvement, when founded on facts and confirmed by experience.[7]

---

[7] J. A. Green, editor. *Pestalozzi's Educational Writings* (New York: Longmans, Green & Co., 1912), pp. 229-32. Used by permission of David McKay Company, Inc.

"Art and Objects of Art,"
Education of Man

Friedrich Froebel, remembered primarily as the initiator of the kindergarten, was born in Thuringia on April 21, 1782, and died on June 21, 1852. After working with Pestalozzi at Yverdon for two years, Froebel studied natural sciences at Göttingen and Berlin. Froebel placed much importance on the early education of children. His main educational idea was that man was action-oriented and he learned only by doing. His *Education of Man* deals primarily with the education of children to the age of seven.

If what has been said heretofore concerning the objective and central points, or axes, of human life is surveyed from a common point of view, human aims will present themselves under three aspects. There is either a tendency to inward repose and life, or a tendency to the study and comprehension of the external, or a tendency to direct representation of the internal.

The first is the prevailing tendency of religion; the second, of the contemplation of nature; the third, of self-development and self-contemplation.

Similarly, it will be found that *mathematics* is concerned more with the representation of the external in the internal, with the representation of inner conformity to universal law, with the representation of nature in inner (human) terms. For this reason mathematics mediates between nature and man; it has reference more to the understanding.

23

Language is concerned more with the outward representation of inner perception, has reference more to reason. There is still wanting for the complete representation of his nature as a whole the representation of inner life as such, of the mind. This representation of the internal, of the inner man as such, is accomplished in *art*.

With one exception all human ideas are relative; mutual relations connect all ideas, and they are distinct only in their terminal points.

Therefore, there is in art, too, a side where it touches mathematics, the understanding; another where it touches the world of language, reason; a third where — although itself clearly a representation of the inner — it coincides with the representation of nature; and a fourth where it coincides with religion.

Yet all these relationships will have to be disregarded, when it is considered with reference to the education of man, in order to lead him to an appreciation of art. Here, art will be considered only in its ultimate unity as the pure representation of the inner. We notice at once that art, or the representation of inner life in art, must be differentiated in accordance with the material it uses.

Now, the material, as an earthly phenomenon, may be motion as such, but audible in sound, as tones which vanish while being produced; or it may be visible in lines, surfaces, and colors, or it may be corporeal, massive. Here, too, as in all actual things, there are, however, many transitions and combinations.

Art, as representation by tones, is music, particularly song. Art, as representation by color, is painting. Art, as representation by plastic material, is modeling. The last two are connected by drawing. This, however, may be considered simply as representation by lines, so that painting would appear as representation by surfaces, and modeling as representation by solids.

On account of the mediating quality of drawing, it appears very early as a phase in human development, and we noticed that even at an earlier stage children have the desire to draw. Even the desire to express ideas by modeling and coloring is frequently found at this earlier stage of childhood, certainly at the very beginning of the stage of boyhood.

This proves clearly that art and appreciation of art constitute a general capacity or talent of man, and should be cared for early, at the latest in boyhood.

This does not imply that the boy is to devote himself chiefly to art and is to become an artist; but that he should be enabled to understand and appreciate works of art. At the same time, a true scholastic education will be sure to guard him against the error of claiming to be an artist, unless there is in him the true artistic calling.

A universal and comprehensive plan of human education must, therefore, necessarily consider at an early period singing, drawing, painting, and modeling; it will not leave them to an arbitrary, frivolous whimsicalness, but treat them as serious objects of the school. Its intention will not be to make each pupil an artist in some one or all of the arts, but to secure to each human being full and all-sided development, to enable him to see man in the universality and all-sided energy of his nature, and, particularly, to enable him to understand and appreciate the products of true art.

Like drawing, but in a different respect, representation in rhythmic speech is mediatory. As representation of the ideal world in language, as the condensed representation, as it were, of the etheral spiritual world of ideas, as the tranquil representation of absolute, eternally moving, and moved life, it belongs to art.

In everything, in life and religion, hence also in art, the ultimate and supreme aim is the clear representation of man as such. In its tendency, Christian art is the highest, for it aims to represent in everything, particularly in and through man, the eternally permanent, the divine. Man is the highest object of human art.

Thus, we have indicated in their totality the object, the aim, and the meaning of human life, as they are revealed even in the life of the boy as a scholar. It still remains to consider the sequences and connections in the development of successive phases of his nature at the scholastic stage, as well as the character, the order, and form of the instruction by which the school seeks to aid the boy in this development.[8]

---

[8]Friedrich Froebel, *The Education of Man,* translated by W. N. Hailmann (New York: D. Appleton and Co., 1887), V. D. 84 & 85, pp. 225-9.

Excerpt, "Vocal Music," *Eighth Annual Report of the Board of Education*

Horace Mann, known as the "Father of the Common Schools," was born at Franklin, Massachusetts on May 4, 1796. He studied law at Brown University and was a practising lawyer until his appointment as the first secretary of the Massachusetts Board of Education. His series of annual reports prompted a new concern for and general improvement in education in Massachusetts, directly, and, indirectly, in the rest of the United States. This reading represents the first official governmental concern with the teaching of music in tax-supported schools of the United States. Upon his resignation as secretary, in 1848, he served in the U. S. House of Representatives and, from 1853 to the time of his death, 1859, he was the president of Antioch College of Ohio.

The preädaptation of the human mind to seek and to find pleasure in Music, is proved by the universality with which the vocal art has been practised among men. Each nation and each age steps forward as a witness, to prove the existence of musical faculties and desires, in the race; and their testimony is so unanimous and cumulative that no tribunal can withstand its force. In cultivating music, therefore, are we not following one of the plainest and most universal indications of nature; or rather of that Being by whose wisdom and benevolence nature was constituted? . . .

Nature not only points, as with her finger, towards the universal culture of the musical art, but she has bestowed upon all men the

means of cultivating it. The voice and the ear are universal endow-
ments; . . . Substantially then, the voice and the ear are universal en-
dowments of nature, and thus the means of enjoying the delights and
of profiting by the utilities of music, are conferred upon all.

. . . the pleasure resulting from the use of the human voice in song,
is the common patrimony of mankind. The inmate of the lowliest
dwelling as well as the master of the lordliest castle may enjoy them.
He whose hard lot deprives him not only of the embellishments but
even of the common comforts of life, may regale himself with the
unpurchased "wealth of song." The pleasures of music attend their
possessor not only in the hours of prosperity, but in those of sorrow.
Music may be a companion in the lone vigils of pain, or in the deeper
solitude of bereavement. It may support and console, when no other
of the benignant family of the Arts could give balm or anodyne to the
wounded spirit.

. . . When the energies of the intellect have been destroyed by a
weight of cares, or its vigor broken down by sickness, — when, from
any cause, these onward-tending faculties can no longer find or create
their natural diversions, it is then, that the simple and calm delights
of music restore the energies that have been wasted by toil, revivify
the spirits languishing with care, or cause the dawn of joy to arise
upon the long watches of sickness. There is not a condition of prosperity or of adversity, in human life, to which something cannot be
found, in the wide compass of music, at once responsive and grateful.
There is not a capacity in the nature of man so pure or lofty, that
music is uncongenial to its exercise, nor a susceptibility so tender and
delicate, as not to welcome its companionship. . . .

There is still another attribute or quality of music too important to
be unnoticed in developing its relations to mankind. It does not require
any degree of perfection as a science, in order to become pleasing as
an art. Doubtless in this, as in all other things, those who possess the
art at all, realize an enjoyment fully proportioned to the degree of art
they possess. . . .

The universal practice of music in most of the schools of the German
states, for a long series of years, is an experiment sufficient of itself to
settle the question of its utility. Probably it is not the least efficient
among the means by which the schools of Prussia are kept in such ad-
mirable order, with so rare a resort to corporal punishment. In that
kingdom no person could be approved as a teacher, — no individual,
indeed, would ever think of presenting himself as a candidate for
teaching, even in the obscurest school and at the lowest salary, — who

was not master both of the theory and practice of vocal music, and also a performer upon one or more instruments. . . .

But to be more specific in presenting the claims of this subject to the attention of our community, I may say,

1st. That Vocal Music promotes health. It accomplishes this object *directly,* by the exercise which it gives to the lungs and other vital organs; and *indirectly,* by the cheerfulness and genial flow of spirits, which it is the especial prerogative of music to bestow. . . .

2nd. Vocal music furnishes the means of intellectual exercises. . . .

3rd. But the social and moral influences of music far transcend, in value, all its physical or intellectual utilities. It holds a natural relationship or affinity with peace, hope, affection, generosity, charity, devotion. There is also a natural repugnance between music and fear, envy, malevolence, misanthropy. . . .

But, grant the expediency of introducing vocal music into our Common Schools, and the question arises, what measures can be adopted to accomplish that end? Unhappily, there are but few persons in our community competent to teach the art even of vocal music. We are an un-musical, — not to say, an anti-musical people. . . .

In our large cities and towns, it is obvious, that there is sufficient pecuniary ability to employ a teacher of music expressly for the schools. . . . In most cases, with competent teachers, music would nearly or quite supersede the necessity of coercion, and thus work a vast economy of blows and tears. But where music has been taught to the pupils by a master of the art, the teacher, though not an adept himself, can superintend the exercises, and thus make it an auxiliary in the government of his school. . . .

But suppose teacher and pupil to be alike incompetent to give lessons, the cases will not be infrequent, where some gentleman or lady, belonging to the school district, will be sufficiently conversant with the art, to give instruction in it. In such a case, it would be a most benevolent and kindly office, if such a person would statedly or occasionally visit the school, and impart the knowledge unattainable from any other source. . . .

A question is sometimes asked, whether, if music cannot be taught scientifically, in our schools, it would be expedient to have it taught by rote. The answer to this question is found in the fact, that most if not all the social and moral effects of music will be realized, when it is practised as an art, as fully as though it were studied as a science. Its adaptation to the intellect depends on its scientific relations; its adaptation to the universal heart of mankind depends on its power to soothe, to tranquilize, or to enliven; to express the highest and most rapturous joys which ever thrill the human soul, or to pour a delicious oblivion over the wounded spirit.[9]

[9]Horace Mann, "Vocal Music," *Eighth Annual Report of the Board of Education, together with the Eighth Annual Report of the Secretary of the Board* (Boston, Dutton and Wentworth, 1845), pp. 117-36.

Excerpt, "What Knowledge Is of Most Worth," *Education: Intellectual, Moral, and Physical*

Herbert Spencer, son of a school teacher, was born in Derby, England, on April 27, 1820. Largely self-educated, he reflected the Victorian optimism of his times. Advocating the importance of the individual over society and science over relation, he eventually developed what he called *The Synthetic Philosophy* which viewed the principle of change as being from homogeneity to heterogenity. His ideas on evolution were published before Darwin's, but he later accepted Darwin's views. It was he who coined the phrase, "survival of the fittest." Spencer held that society exists for the benefit of the individual — it is this individualism which is the key to all of his thinking. Spencer died before he could finish the publication of *The Synthetic Philosophy* on December 8, 1903.

And now we come to that remaining division of human life which includes the relaxations, pleasures, and amusements filling leisure hours. After considering what training best fits for self-preservation, for the obtainment of sustenance, for the discharge of parental duties, and for the regulation of social and political conduct; we have now to consider what training best fits for the miscellaneous ends not included in these —for the enjoyments of Nature, of Literature, and of the Fine Arts, in all their forms. Postponing them as we do to things that bear more vitally upon human welfare; and bringing everything, as we have, to the test of actual value; it will perhaps be inferred that we are inclined to slight these less essential things. No greater mistake could be made, however. We yield to none in the value we attach to aesthetic culture and its pleasures. Without painting, sculpture, music, poetry, and the emotions produced by natural beauty of every kind, life would lose half its charm. So far from thinking that the training and gratification of the tastes are unimportant, we believe the time will come when they will occupy a much larger share of human life than now. When the forces of Nature have been fully conquered to man's use — when the means of production have been brought to perfection — when labour has been economized to the highest degree — when education has been so systemized that a preparation for the more essential activities may be made with comparative rapidity — and when, consequently, there is a great increase of spare time; then will the poetry, both of Art and Nature, rightly fill a large space in the minds of all.

But it is one thing to admit that aesthetic culture is in a high degree conducive to human happiness; and another thing to admit that it is a fundamental requisite to human happiness. However important it may be, it must yield precedence to those kinds of culture which bear more directly upon the duties of life. As before hinted, literature and the fine arts are made possible by those activities which make individual and social life possible; and manifestly, that which is made possible, must be postponed to that which makes it possible. A florist cultivates a plant for the sake of its flower; and regards the roots and leaves as of value, chiefly because they are instrumental in producing the flower. But while, as an ultimate product, the flower is the thing to which everything else is subordinate, the florist very well knows that the root and leaves are intrinsically of greater importance; because on them the evolution of the flower depends. He bestows every care in rearing a healthy plant; and knows it would be folly if, in his anxiety to obtain the flower, he were to neglect the plant. Similarly in the case before us. Architecture, sculpture, painting, music, poetry, etc., may be truly called the efflorescence of civilized life. But even supposing them to be of such transcendent worth as to subordinate the civilized life out of which they grow (which can hardly be asserted), it will still be admitted that the production of a healthy civilized life must be the first consideration; and that the knowledge conducing to this must occupy the highest place.

And here we see most distinctly the vice of our educational system. It neglects the plant for the sake of the flower. In anxiety for elegance, it forgets substance. While it gives no knowledge conducive to self-preservation — while of knowledge that facilitates gaining a livelihood it gives but the rudiments, and leaves the greater part to be picked up any how in after life — while for the discharge of parental functions it makes not the slightest provision — and while for the duties of citizenship it prepares by imparting a mass of facts, most of which are irrelevant, and the rest without a key; it is diligent in teaching every thing that adds to refinement, polish, éclat. However fully we may admit that extensive acquaintance with modern languages is a valuable accomplishment, which, through reading, conversation, and travel, aids in giving a certain finish; it by no means follows that this result is rightly purchased at the cost of that vitally important knowledge sacrificed to it. Supposing it true that classical education conduces to elegance and correctness of style; it cannot be said that elegance and correctness of style are comparable in importance to a familiarity with the principles that should guide the rearing of children. Grant that the taste may be greatly improved by reading all the poetry written in extinct languages; yet it is not to be inferred that such improvement of taste is equivalent in value to an acquaintance with the laws of health. Accomplishments, the fine arts, *belles-lettres,* and all those things which, as we say, constitute the efflorescence of civilization, should be wholly subordinate to that knowledge and discipline in which civilization rests. *As they occupy the leisure part of life, so should they occupy the leisure part of education.*[10]

---

[10]Herbert Spencer, *Education: Intellectual, Moral, and Physical* (New York: D. Appleton and Co., 1861), pp. 71-5.

Excerpt, "The Relation of National Ethics to National Arts"

John Ruskin, English social reformer, art critic, and essayist, was born in London on February 8, 1819. Educated at Oxford and later holder of the Slade Professorship there, he turned out a prodigious amount of writing during his lifetime. Later in life Ruskin suffered a complete mental breakdown, he recovered sufficiently to write again, but gave up his teaching duties. Ruskin died on January 20, 1900.

. . . There is, indeed, an absolute right and wrong in art (the doubt of these has been the chief cause of our failures and errors). There is right painting, and wrong painting; right music, and wrong music; right gesture, and wrong gesture. . . . And this is the great practical truth which I desire to bring before you to-day. We cannot teach art as an abstract skill or power. It is the result of a certain ethical state in the nation, and at full period of the national growth that efflorescence of its ethical state will infallibly be produced: be it bad or good, we can no more teach nor shape it than we can streak an orchard blossom with strange colours or infuse into its fruit a juice it has not drawn out of the sap. And, farther, such seed of art as we sow, such also must we reap; that which is born of lasciviousness begets lasciviousness, that which is shed from folly will spring up into folly, and that which is sown of truth bear fruit of truth, according to the ground it is cast on, some thirty-fold, some sixty, some an hundred.

. . . Wherever the intellect of a people is perfectly aroused, art must exist; and, when it exists, every failure in the beauty of it is the sure and proportioned sign of an ethical depravity. Nor is it either a question whether art be an important part of the human energy or not; small or great, it is a necessary part.

And thus it is true of all the arts from the least to the greatest that they spring from the whole humanity, and that their object is the whole humanity. . . . Therefore whatever art, whatever thing we have to teach, we can only teach hopefully by having first a right conception of the whole humanity, . . .

.   .   .   .

Now, Music rightly so called is the expression of the joy or grief of noble minds for noble causes. . . . I say then that true music is the natural and necessary expression of a kingly, holy passion for a lofty cause; that, in proportion to the royalty and force of our personality, the nature and expression of its joy or suffering becomes measured, chastened, calm, and capable of interpretation only by the majesty of ordered, beautiful, and worded sound. Exactly in proportion to the degree in which we become narrow in the cause and conception of our passions, incontinent in the utterance of them, feeble of perseverance in them, sullied or shameful in the indulgence of them, their expression by musical sound becomes broken, mean, fatuitous, and at last impossible; the measured waves of the air of heaven will not lend themselves to expression of ultimate vice, it must be for ever sunk into discordance or silence. And since, as before stated, every work of right art has a tendency to reproduce the ethical state which first developed it, this, which of all the arts is most directly ethical in origin, is also the most direct in power of discipline; the first, the simplest, the most effective of all instruments of moral instruction; while in the failure and betrayal of its function, it becomes the subtlest aid of moral degradation.

I say failure rather than disease of function. For, strictly speaking, the distinction is not between good music and bad music, but between that which is and is not music. And so in all the other arts, strictly speaking, there is no such thing as bad sculpture or bad painting. There is only no sculpture and no painting. . . . The distinction therefore between the natures of exalting and of corrupting music, which the Greeks mythically expressed by the contest between Apollo and Marsyas, and between the Muses and the Sirens, does not depend so much on an actual difference in essence as on a different ethical subordination. In good music the pleasure received by the ear is wholly subordinate to the purpose of expression. . . . And the worst corruption of music in modern days is not in, as it might at first be supposed, the exaltation of a dangerous sentiment by faithful sound, as in the hymn of the Marseillaise, but it is the idle and sensual seeking for pleasure in the sound only, without any true purpose of sentiment at all, and often without the slightest effort to discern the composer's intention, or understand the relation in a master's work between the syllable and the note. There is no harm but a real discipline in the purposeful expression of any sentiment which can be set to noble sound. But there is infinite harm in an idle and wanton catching of pleasant cadences with only foolish meaning in them, or none.

. . . Thus many people imagine that when they are drawn by their delight in the higher forms of musical composition to withdraw themselves for a time from common life and solemnize their hearts by hearing sacred words beautifully sung, there is, at least in the degree in which their true sympathies may be excited, a gain to their moral character. Nay, many of them would probably assure us, and with perfect truth, that they distinctly felt themselves morally stronger and purer after such pleasure. But that greater strength of the soul, though actual and undeniable for the time, is a dearly purchased gain; it is just what the increase of strength by over-exciting stimulant is to the body, and the morbid and momentary increase of moral sentiment is necessarily followed by general dullness of the moral nerve. . . .

It is not a good thing for a weak and wicked person to be momentarily touched or charmed by sacred art. It is a deadly thing for them to indulge in the habitual enjoyment of it. The *Miserere* of the Sistine sends every one home in a degree hardened, who did not come there to ask for mercy; and the daily chanted praise of the cathedral choir leaves every one who comes not to adore daily less capable of adoration. And as it is with the religious feelings, so in all others capable of being expressed by sound. If you have them, and desire truly to utter them, music becomes the most perfect utterance; for it is only noble life which can be so expressed. Envy, avarice, malice, cannot be written in music, but loyalty can, and love; and righteous anger and faith, courage and compassion, pure childish cheerfulness, and childish peace; only in these delicate passions and in the earnest disciplines of life can we learn to enter into the chastened sweetness and the ordered perfectness of sound. What remnant of the faculty of pity, of justice, of spiritual joy or grief, there may be left in us, we may by such sounds exalt, if we desire truly to exalt them; but if we seek only the pleasure of the sense, then the music searches for the dregs of good in our spiritual being, and wrings them forth, and drinks them; . . .[11]

---

[11]E. T. Cook and Alexander Wedderburn, editors, *The Works of John Ruskin* (New York: Longmans, Green, and Co., Ltd., 1905), Vol. XIX, pp. 166-180.

"Music and Education: The Place of Music in Humane Letters"

ↄↄↄↄↄↄↄↄ

William Henry Hadow was born on December 27, 1859. His great contribution to music was through his critical writings. Hadow spent a lifetime of teaching and administering collegiate education in England. It was through his efforts that music secured an acknowledged place in the English school curriculum. The following essay points up his beliefs on that score. It is also interesting to note that this essay and two others were first delivered as lectures at the Rice Institute, Houston, Texas, on December 7, 8, and 9, 1926. Hadow died in London on April 8, 1937.

We have seen how large a part can be played in the training of intellect and character by a careful, selective study of language and of the great literatures of which it is the expression. Among such languages I claim a high place for the language of music: among such literatures for musical composition. It follows, therefore, that I should indicate the grounds on which this claim can be made good, and the practical method by which its requirements can be satisfied. The case is one of such inherent truth and justice that if I fail to carry conviction it will be the fault of the advocate.

. . . .

Here, then, is a field of educational reform, that we should admit musical history to the same place in our annals which we now accord to the history of literature. Our culture is "like an ill-roasted egg, all on one side," if we are familiar with Spenser and Shakespeare but not with Byrd and Tallis, with Milton but not with Bach, with Goethe but not with Beethoven: if we can interest ourselves in the vogue of the Elizabethan sonnet but not of the Elizabethan madrigal, and trace the growth of drama or novel without a thought to that of sonata and quartet and symphony. All these claim our investigation: all have borne their part in nurturing the spirit of man: indeed, if there be anything to choose between them we may even maintain that the influence of music has been the more subtle and the more penetrating.

But it is not only or chiefly in virtue of its historical record that the place of music is to be vindicated. This is only preliminary or at any rate ancillary to the study of music itself: to that first-hand knowledge of the composer's work without which the most eloquent commentary is useless. And because this reaches to the very heart of my subject I will ask leave to begin from the first elements, tracing as well as I can the course of the musical education which I have in view, and fitting into my scheme, when the moment comes, the stages which most appropriately belong to institutions of university rank.

Here may be noted a very curious and widespread superstition. Music is written in an alphabet of its own: an alphabet of minims and semiquavers, of sharps and flats and naturals, ruled for convenience on a stave of five lines and punctuated for convenience with a succession of upright bars. Like every other alphabet this is conventional: like every other it has its own system of fixed and determinate symbols, each with a special significance. . . . Like them it has to be learned: when learned it can be read. Yet a vast majority of educated people maintain that the silent reading of music is an impossibility: what they call reading means playing or singing at sight or, in the farthest extreme, following a performance with the score: . . .

. . . To read it silently is usually harder than to read prose or verse because one usually has to co-ordinate a number of different lines, but it is certainly not impossible or unprofitable, for an increasing number of people are doing it with genuine pleasure. . . .

Our ideal education in music should, therefore, begin through the natural avenues of reading and writing. The practice of musical dictation, now customary in many English schools, is the method to be employed: after acquiring the first alphabetical rudiments the child writes down a melody which it has just heard, or conversely, sings or plays a melody which it has just seen on the blackboard. In both cases the tune, whether apprehended through the eye or the ear, has to be swiftly memorized and it is remarkable in how short a time the exercise can be done with sureness and accuracy. At first only short and simple phrases are used (it would be the same with any other dictation); these can be extended as time goes on and experience matures: it is of further assistance to let the pupil learn pieces by heart and read them silently while they are still familiar; and in this way proceeding step by step from known to unknown it is possible to bring the faculties of sight and hearing into a very efficient co-ordination.

From the outset children should be accustomed to hear well-selected examples of the best music, and of the best alone. The ideal way of presenting these is that a competent teacher should play them with a running commentary pointing out not some fantastic conjecture as to their poetic meaning, but their felicities of phrase and melody and harmonic texture, of colour and surprise and climax, of coherent stanza and organic structural form. . . . The two most famous of all educators have laid it down as a principle that children should be protected from every degrading sight or sound: discrimination comes with growth of years and maturity of judgment, and is far more likely to be rightly exercised if it is founded on a solid tradition of excellence. Much of the so-called music which is written for schools is wholly unworthy of its place: without purity, without talent, without significance, securing its place apparently by accident and keeping it by mere carelessness and apathy. For there is nothing in the world to which we apply a less effective standard than to music. I do not believe that people prefer the worse: they are ready enough to discard it when their attention is engaged: for the most part they listen in contented indifference which it requires a dynamic shock to disturb. . . .

.   .   .   .

At some stage in musical education, and probably at this period of school life, there should be some systematic drill in the elements of theory. It is of great assistance afterwards to know such technical terms as designate ordinary matters of fact, and though in music these are mostly dull and uninspiring, they are not many in number and are not difficult to learn. . . . Most important of all, because vital to the understanding of the larger classics, is a study of the chief architectural forms in music: mass and madrigal, opera and oratorio, suite, partita, and overture, the fugue and all that it implies, the complex organism of sonata and quartet and symphony. These form the very plot and ground plan of all musical composition: if we do not understand their principles we are like a theatre-audience to whom the whole construction of the play should be unintelligible; and though we may in such a case get some momentary entertainment from particular actions or episodes, it is no paradox to hold that we are less favourably placed than our neighbour who knows the language.

It is an arguable question how far the students whom we have chiefly in view — those who are taking music as part of a liberal education — should be encouraged to play on instruments or to compose. Of the two I incline to lay stress on the latter. Many more people have an aptitude for it than is commonly supposed; and even if the results are of no great value the attempt to produce them is abundantly rewarded by a quickened sensibility and a more intelligent appreciation: . . . Solo playing I should discourage except in cases of real aptitude, but all who can should take part in the practices of the school orchestra and the pieces should be adapted so as to admit of as many recruits as possible. Above all, choral singing should be universal. The cultivation of the solo voice is best deferred until after the period of adolescence: a period at the beginning of every day should be set aside for class-singing, not only because it is a delight in itself, but because it is the best of preparations for the work that is to come after. . . .

For this purpose two books are required: a collection of hymns and a collection of secular songs. Both should be specially edited by the best panel of judges available — it would be an easy matter to choose such a panel in this country — and kept on the highest level of words and music without favour or compromise. . . .

We are now in a position to consider the end and aim towards which this address has been directed — the assignment of music to its proper place in the studies of a university or of an institution of university rank. Ideally speaking, we should presuppose that before this stage is reached the ground which we have already surveyed should have been traversed; that the student as he approaches this threshold should bring with him a general school education in music and some knowledge both of the outline of its history and of the elementary principles of its structure. . . .

In whatever way the elements have been acquired it is on their foundation that the university course should be built. For this the personnel and equipment can be easily stated, and, in a country so generous to education as America, should not be difficult to provide.

. . . .

The cardinal object of such a department is to train the listener. Students who show special capacity as executants or composers may be given every facility for instruction and practice: they correspond to students in other departments who have a talent for research; but the curriculum should be so framed and the courses of teaching and examination so devised that they are within the grasp of any one who loves music and who is prepared to give the requisite time and care to its comprehension. . . . The study of musical texts, with the theoretic and historic background which they imply, should be one of the recognized options of the curriculum and, at any rate in arts and pure science, should have equal citizenship with all other options.[12]

[12]W. H. Hadow, *Collected Essays* (London: Oxford University Press, 1928), pp. 272-89. Permission to reprint granted by the publisher.

"Musical Art and the Public,"
Eurhythmics, Art, and Education

Émile Jaques-Dalcroze, born in Vienna on July 6, 1865, is chiefly noted for his system of music teaching known as eurhythmics. This is a system which utilizes bodily movement as its main approach to the subject. Although, outwardly, it is a physical technique, the mental is in complete control for it must react to the rhythmic dictates of the music and then transmit to the motor the appropriate physical responses. It is now employed in only isolated instances although the system received much attention throughout the Western world from around 1900 to about 1940. Jaques-Dalcroze died in Geneva, Switzerland on July 1, 1950.

Public taste is formed as the result of habits which people have contracted through institutions. When these are of but little interest, protests are raised in the name of art and in every town or city that claims to be a centre of art, there springs into being a whole series of small clans, each of which discusses in its own special manner the bad taste shown by such institutions. These small clans are not without their use. In the very heart of traditions regarding a style which is not above suspicion they keep alive the respect of what has been, or at all events of what should have been; they are guardians of a past, whether real or illusory; even heralds of a possible future. Unfortunately they cannot agree with one another and so have no direct influence on the artistic development of the people. The fact is they are not themselves prepared for their mission. They have not received the education suitable to them, the *clan education*. I will explain:

Artistic progress depends on education, and each personality, each group of individuals, each association of groups, needs special education. Every one of us is an echo of his environment, every artistic action is a product of the spirit of the age. Of course, genius alone can effect progress. But genius is the apanage of individuals; if it is to influence the speedy progress of the entire community it needs to be backed by groupings of talented artists. And these artists will exercise effective influence on the public only when they consent to submit to education by the strongest personalities. If every artist and association of artists looked upon artistic traditions as a precious heritage to be handed on to the young in the best possible condition and not deteriorated by use, artistic progress would be no empty word. However divergent the opinions of talented individuals, if their object is to develop public taste, they must combine in protesting against everything calculated to corrupt mankind. Once bad habits have been suppressed, it will be time to discuss the choice to be made between new habits of a different kind. Above all, scorn of everything ugly must be instilled in the mind of the public, and desire for perfection must take its place.

It is advisable to appeal to feeling, not to knowledge. Instruction is but little; education is everything. The first step along the path of regeneration is taken when we feel harassed by a desire to destroy those evil habits that constitute a barrier to progress. Nevertheless, it is clearly not sufficient to be able to destroy; it is not enough to cultivate the imagination. We must also know how to create anew. Then only is there room for instruction. Unfortunately it appears as though instruction, almost everywhere, takes precedence over education. The school attempts to instill knowledge, not to create opinions. And when some individual creates a trend of opinion the latter is seldom of general interest. Is it not indispensable that artists desirous of the progress of their country, instead of flaring abroad "art-principle rockets," should endeavor to set up "opinion-standards," to establish "aesthetical-law foundations," and to scatter among the public "beauty-idea seeds"? And to effect this, a temporary sacrifice of private opinions is needed since public taste evolves but slowly. Still, no sooner have general opinions become habitual than victory is ours, and then we have to think of propounding to the masses such modifications as they would have been unable to appreciate at the outset for want of a starting-point and through lack of conviction in the first instance.

Very many lovers of music have not sufficient *naïveté*. They go to concerts, not in order to feel musical emotions, but rather for the purpose of analysing musical processes and having the satisfaction of criticising them from a personal point of view. Instead of obeying their temperament, they listen to their reason. Instead of expanding, they contract. A musical production, however, is not a scientific thesis which can be read again and again at one's leisure and coldly analysed. Music acts on the whole of the organism like a magic force which suppresses the understanding and irresistibly takes possession of the entire being. To insist on analysing this force is to destroy its very essence. Every public body is made up both of the analytical and of the receptive. The majority of the latter are paralysed by a sort of instinctive shame created in them by age-long traditions of personal control and subjugation, of physical restraint, which may perhaps give them superior moral force, though they are thereby prevented from being frankly artists and from revealing the deep impression conveyed to the whole nature of man by the divine influence of music.

It is this feeling of shame that makes so many people prefer the stereotyped playing of works by Beethoven and Bach to freer interpretations which retain their sensorial character and restore the original impulsive life of the individual soul — this feeling, too, that causes them to prefer exhibitions of sheer virtuosity; for by public appreciation of such playing they do not compromise their inner self and yet they satisfy the scientific nature, that of every race which appreciates above all the qualities of order and style in music.

Still, this shame is noble in its essence and is calculated to act as a counterpoise to exaggerations in nuance, to strivings after external effects, to those cravings after pathetism which compromise the cause of music in too many superior minds. We have, on the other hand, the snobs, who manifest no shame of any kind, who testify to their swollen vanity by futile and noisy prattling, who say they are moved when they are not, who pretend to detest the very thing which has no existence so far as they are concerned, and all the time, while claiming that they hold the musical art in honour, merely practice the art of falsehood and deceit.

Between music and the public there should exist the closest collaboration. If sound reaches the human heart without being able to enter and find its abode therein, that is due to lack of musical temperament. But if, from a desire to appear sensitive, the human heart merely pretends to respond to the beneficent influence of music, then we have hypocrisy. Snobbery, while seeming to favour progress, merely causes misunderstandings, worries and annoys intelligent and sincere people, and hinders the natural development of art. It substitutes artifice for reality, contrasts imitation with nature, and replaces the genuine savour of good taste by an apparent elegance and enthusiasm.

Apart, however, from the analytical and the scientific, the shy and the snobs, there are still to be found many sensitive and thoroughly sincere individuals, enamoured of the ideal, true advocates of art and progress. Have they sufficient influence to develop the artistic sense of the people, direct their judgment, give full opportunity to their creative faculties and refine the style of their interpretations? Of course, if they could unite and protest against the evil habits acquired, if they could force the snobs to check their untimely ardour, the shy not to fear to reveal the *naïveté* of their mental state, the analytical to reconcile exigencies of style with those of temperament. . . . But the one thing to remember is that, instead of indulging in selfish enjoyment of music, they should devote themselves to spreading a taste for it in every class of society, remembering that Spencer looked upon a rational and experimental education, beginning at school, as capable of utterly changing the artistic mentality of a people within forty years.[13]

[13]E. Jaques-Dalcroze, *Eurhythmics, Art, and Education,* translated by Frederick Rothwell, Cynthia Cox, editor. (New York: A. S. Barnes & Co., 1930), pp. 239-43. Permission to reprint granted by the publishers.

Part II

RESEARCH

Maturation and Music

Human behavior is more dependent upon learning and less regulated by instinct than that of lower animals. Also, the range, as well as the variation, of behavior of man is far greater than that of lower animals. Man is born into this world with but a few behavioral responses and these are innate. However, man is born with the capacity to respond. This capacity to respond is totally dependent upon the accumulation of experience for development and refinement. This is accomplished through the adaptive process. Therefore, man's environment, much of which is the development and refinement of preceding man's behavior — this aspect of environment is called culture — has a great deal to do with the extent to which he develops his capacity to respond. Since culture, which is a pattern of behavior, is cumulative, that is, passed from person to person and from generation to generation, it is necessary to establish a means, formal or informal, to develop and refine behavior according to the dictates of that culture, or pattern. There is research which indicates the critical period of development and refinement of behavior is very early in life. Too, research in human development is very positive in its indication of the need for the development and refinement of behavior, that is, education of the young. This most obvious generalization includes, of course, musical behavior. It is possible for man to achieve a maximum of flexibility in his behavior; however, research also shows that this requires a prolonged childhood experience of a type which develops this flexibility. (See the *Developmental Chart* at the end of this section.)

Physical Development

The research literature in educational psychology, as well as music psychology, points out, numerous times, that musical responsiveness is, in part, dependent on the physical development of the student. The pioneer research in human growth and development was directed by such individuals as Shirley,[1] Terman,[2] Halverson,[3] McGraw,[4] and Rothney.[5] Their research was primarily concerned with the influence of nature and nurture upon the growth and development of children. The battle is still raging. Suffice it to say, if the maximum conditions of nature and nurture are not present, maximum growth and development will not take place. One of the best sources providing information on almost all aspects of human development is the inventory by Berelson and Steiner.[6] Although this work deals with the subject of general human behavior rather than specific musical behavior, it, nevertheless, establishes a basis from which more specific studies can be developed. Their summarization of research on gross abilities (e.g., crawling, grasping, walking, climbing, etc.) shows that first occurrence is almost entirely dependent on maturation rather than on experience.[7] There are other research reports in this work which deal with muscular development, with the appearance sequences of motor skills, and the approximate ages at which these skills first become evident. By and large, the sequence of development is the same for all children. Almost all of the research indicates that a common age at which various functions typically emerge is fairly predictable. The individual differences occur in the rate of development rather than in the sequence of development.[8] The child experiencing a faster development rate tends to retain his advantage in that area of development over his slower counterpart. As children grow older, their behavior becomes more differentiated in perception, in response to environment, in thought processes, and in emotional reaction.

---

[1]M. M. Shirley, *The First Two Years* (Minneapolis: University of Minnesota Press, 1933).

[2]Lewis M. Terman, *Mental and Physical Traits of a Thousand Gifted Children,* Vol. 1 of *Genetic Studies of Genius* (Palo Alto: Stanford University Press, 1925).

[3]H. M. Halverson, *An Experimental Study of Prehension in Infants* (Genetic Psychology Monographs, X/2 and 3, 1931).

[4]M. S. McGraw, *Growth: A Study of Johnny and Jimmy* (New York: D. Appleton-Century Co., 1935).

[5]J. W. M. Rothney, "Recent Findings in the Study of the Physical Growth of Children" (*Journal of Educational Research,* XXXV/3, 1941).

[6]Bernard Berelson and Gary A. Steiner, *Human Behavior: An Inventory of Scientific Findings* (New York: Harcourt, Brace & World, Inc., 1964).

[7]*Ibid.,* p. 57.

[8]*Ibid.,* p. 51.

Closely related to the problem of rate and sequence development is the Boardman research concerning the effect of preschool training on vocal accuracy.[9] Her subjects — for the purpose of the investigation — children ranging from kindergarten age through the second-grade age, were divided into two groups: (a) those receiving skill training in vocal accuracy and (b) those receiving no skill training. Her conclusion was that preschool training may accelerate normal development of vocal accuracy, but will not noticeably affect it in any other way. Both groups experienced a gradual increase, from one grade level to another, in the total number of accurate responses. The conclusion of this research is consistent with the conclusions of other research in the general area of development, indicating, in the learning of complex skills or other accomplishments requiring training, that practice is most effective at the point of maturation — not before, but also, not long after, the period of physical readiness. Having mentioned practice in the learning process, it is well to point out that, usually, practice separated by rest periods contributes more to the efficiency of learning than do longer periods of uninterrupted practice. The Childs research,[10] comparing two methods of beginning instrumental music instruction, seems to affirm this principle.

Music skills, such as learning to perform on a musical instrument, rhythmic action, and singing, are related to the general physical-motor development of the physique. As in the gross-skill development of the body, motor development results from both structural maturation and learning opportunity. The child's physical and social environment apparently exerts considerable influence on the extensity of the motor skill development. Jones,[11] in affirmation of the preceding statement, concluded from her study of childhood motor development that minimum performance of motor skills is dependent upon an appropriate degree of neuromuscular maturation, however, the development of the skill into a graceful, coordinated performance is dependent upon continued practice. Also, the merging of activities, which previously were accomplished as separate performances, seemed to begin as soon as each activity had reached a stage at which the child's complete attention was not required for his performance.

---

[9]Eunice L. Boardman, *An Investigation of the Effect of Preschool Training on the Development of Vocal Accuracy in Young Children* (unpublished doctoral dissertation, University of Illinois, 1964 — *Dissertation Abstracts,* XXV/2/1245).

[10]Carroll A. Childs, *A Comparison of Two Distributed Instructional Periods in the Teaching of Beginning Instrumental Music Students* (unpublished doctoral dissertation, Colorado State College, 1963 — *Dissertation Abstracts,* XX/1/517).

[11]Theresa D. Jones, *The Development of Certain Motor Skills and Play Activities in Young Children* (Child Development Monographs, 26, 1939).

A study of the available research on motor skill development would solve a number of teaching problems for the in-service music teacher. It is, for example, important to the music teacher to know whether or not special practice will develop skills beyond the maturational level of the individual student. Earlier research indicated there was a rate of development which no amount of practice could change. The implication, to the music teacher, being that music skills and techniques taught to the child before he was ready, physically and psychologically, often develops poor habits and attitudes which are almost impossible to overcome in later years. Later research seems to point to the same conclusion — encouraging children, before the age of physical readiness, may actually retard the development of the skill by impairing the desire and eagerness for learning the skill.

Motor skills seem to develop in this pattern: from two to six years, there is an unevenness of development; at five years, children usually start to skip and dance; from six to eight years, the small muscles have developed sufficiently to do work requiring manual dexterity, such as writing; at ten years, there is a finer development of eye-hand coordination; by age eleven, almost all children have an organized need for strenuous physical activity — children can attain proficiency in certain physical skills; there is a steady improvement of physical coordination during the teens — these are the years for developing the finer motor skills which are demanded for adult living.[12]

Mental Development

Webster's Collegiate Dictionary defines the mind as "that which perceives, wills, thinks, etc. The perceptive and thinking part of consciousness, exclusive of will and emotion." Seashore describes the musical mind as "the possession, in a serviceable degree, of those capacities which are essential for the hearing, the feeling, the understanding, and ordinarily, for some form of expression of music, with a resulting drive or urge toward music."[13] The degree of possession of these attributes could be termed as one's ability. Also, it is appropriate to quote Farnsworth's summary of Franklin's conclusions: "music ability has two aspects, one being the mechanical-acoustic (e.g., pitch, timbre, time, and intensity discrimination) and the other, on a far higher level

---

[12]Ruth Strang, *An Introduction to Child Study,* 4th ed. (New York: The Macmillan Co., 1959), p. 447.
[13]Carl E. Seashore, *Psychology of Music* (New York: McGraw-Hill Book Co., Inc., 1938), p. 2.

. . . the judicious-musical."[14] Musical mind, musical ability, musical aptitude, music capability are all terms used, in the past, more or less synonymously. "Present-day music educators generally tend to think that musical aptitude is best understood as a product of environmental influences and inherited potential."[15] Just what the relationship between "influences" and "potential" is has been an intriguing problem for researchers.

The early research on the relationship of intelligence and musical ability indicated there was little correlation between the two. Kwalwasser's research inferred this, as did Seashore's.[16] Ross' research on relationships between intelligence, scholastic achievement, and musical talent found a significant correlation between scholastic achievement and musical talent in certain instances; however, the coefficients of correlation were so low one could not be used to predict the other.[17] Ross also pointed out that students, who elected music courses in the last two years of secondary school, were slightly superior in intelligence to the general population to which they belong. These and other first researchers were aware, however, that pupils possessing musical talent in quantity and quality sufficient enough to be classified as superior in musical ability were also superior in intelligence and scholastic achievement.

There have been attempts to isolate attributes or qualities, which, when grouped together, comprise musical ability in order to use the isolated one to predict the whole, or total ability. One such attempt was the Gesler research.[18] Original tests were devised to determine what relationship might exist between pitch discrimination and phonic sensitivity. Her results were not positive enough to establish a valid predictive tool.

---

[14]Paul R. Farnsworth, *The Social Psychology of Music* (New York: The Dryden Press, 1958), p. 181; E. Franklin, *Tonality as a Basis for the Study of Musical Talent* (Goteborg, Sweden: Gumperts Förlag, 1956).

[15]Edwin Gordon, *Manual: Musical Aptitude Profile* (Boston: Houghton Mifflin Co., 1965), p. 1.

[16]Jacob Kwalwasser, "The Composition of Music Ability," *Music Education* (The Thirty-fifth Yearbook of the National Society for the Study of Education, Part II. Bloomington, Ill.: Public School Publishing Co., 1936), pp. 35-42; Carl E. Seashore, "The Discovery and Guidance of Musical Talent," *Educational Diagnosis*. (The Thirty-fourth Yearbook of the National Society for the Study of Education. Bloomington, Ill.: Public School Publishing Co., 1935), pp. 447-461.

[17]Verne Ralph Ross, *Relationships Between Intelligence and Scholastic Achievement and Musical Talent* (Claremont, Calif.: California Bureau of Juvenile Research, 1937).

[18]Harriet L. Gesler, *An Analysis of the Relation Between Pitch Discrimination and Phonic Sensitivity in First Grade Children* (unpublished doctoral dissertation, University of Connecticut, 1958 — *Dissertation Abstracts*, XIX/5/988).

Research by George Kyme demonstrated that aesthetic judgment may serve as a statistically significant tool for the testing of musical ability.[19] He developed a test called the "Test of Esthetic Judgment of Music." The following validity coefficients were obtained when Kyme's test was compared with other tests of musical ability:

Seashore Measures of Musical Talents	.46
Whistler-Thorpe Music Aptitude Test	.19
Kwalwasser-Dykema Music Test	.64
Kyme Test of Esthetic Judgment	.74

Kyme's research on aesthetic judgment reminds one of the Birch research.[20] He simply surveyed the types and numbers of recordings owned by college students with varying musical backgrounds. Some of his conclusions were: at least three years of participation in high school music offerings rendered better taste and discrimination than less than three years of participation; training in vocal music rendered better taste and discrimination than instrumental music training; women have broader tastes than men; high school music study only, and private music study only, render the same taste discrimination, but a combination of the two renders better taste discrimination than one or the other.

Since there is a relationship between verbal aptitude and other aptitudes,[21] it might be productive for music teachers to investigate the research in this field for principles of learning and development which can be applied to the teaching of music. Also, if there is a significant relationship between verbal aptitude and musicality, then there may be the distinct possibility the one might be used to predict the other.

Social-Emotional Development

Of all the arts, music is both an individual and a group activity. It is an obvious fact that socialization, in some form or another, takes place during any group activity. Under the guidance of a competent teacher the social values stemming from participation in music activities can be unlimited. The social aspect of music learning, either in school or out, is often cited as one of the primary purposes for en-

[19]George H. Kyme, "Are Musical Tastes Indicative of Musical Capacity?" (*Journal of Research in Music Education*, IV/1; Spring, 1956), pp. 44-51.
[20]Thomas E. Birch, *Musical Taste as Indicated by Records Owned by College Students with Varying High School Experiences* (unpublished doctoral dissertation, University of Missouri, 1962 — *Dissertation Abstracts*, XIII/7/2545).
[21]Dorothea McCarthy, "Language Development," *Manual of Child Psychology*, Leonard Carmichael, editor. (New York: Wiley, 1946), pp. 476-581.

couraging the child to participate in music activities. There can be little argument that one of the reasons students participate in music activities is the opportunity for contact with other students. Although the social aspect of music should not be the major reason for including music in the curriculum, music teachers should be aware that one of the major purposes of the curriculum is to develop acceptable social values. The music teacher, thus, should possess an understanding of social development, not because music activities fulfill a social function, but because he usually works within the framework of group activity in guiding the music learning process. He must know the degree of social awareness of each individual in his group and that the social awareness of that individual develops from self-centeredness, through family-centeredness, through peer-group centeredness, to community-centeredness.

It is true that music affects the emotions. The ancient Greeks recognized this, and it has been recognized since. Whether this is the primary reason for teaching music, has been and is open for debate. One of the functions of education is to develop the ability to make intelligent decisions — decisions which are based on experience, fact, and reason. Making an intelligent decision is an exercising of the intellect. An emotional decision does not require exercising the intellect; such a decision is not based on experience, fact, and reason. Emotional decisions are irrational as compared to the rational decisions of the intellect. That music can be pleasurable is, also, an acceptable fact. Pleasure, when based on experience, fact, and reason, is intellectually gratifying. Pleasure, when based on a mere "titillation of the senses," is an emotional catharsis — a primitive gratification. Whether the formal educational process should, or should not, be involved in providing for the possibilities of experiencing pleasure can be debated. If that pleasure contributes to the well-being of the person, provides for a more fulfilling life, provides for the satisfaction of the need for beauty, then yes. If that pleasure is only an emotional catharsis, then no. If the results of the teaching of music provide only for an emotional catharsis, then music should be left to the informal, or out-of-school educational process. However, if the school is to teach music, then the teaching of it must be based on the presentation of experience, fact, and reason. The student equipped with musical experience, fact, and reason, can then make an intelligent decision as to whether or not to utilize music as a source and means of experiencing pleasure.

The preceding paragraph does not mean to imply that intellectual pleasure is completely divorced from the emotion. For it is not. An experience which gives pleasure because there is a recognition of past experience, of known facts, and involves a process of reasoning cannot but help to stimulate a sense of emotional well-being. However, this sense of emotional well-being is the more fulfilling and the more satisfying because it calls upon a depth of reaction based upon knowledge. The greater the backlog of experience, the knowledge of fact, and the ability to reason, the greater the intellectual pleasure and, hence, the deeper the emotional pleasure. The music teacher must understand the distinction between intellectual pleasure and emotional pleasure and how the first can enhance and give meaning to the second. He must know that emotional responsiveness develops from the instinctive to the intellectual.

Developmental Chart of Children 5-17*

Age	Physical	Mental	Social-Emotional
5 years Kindergarten	Brain almost fully grown. Little difference in size, weight, coordination, and physical strength of boys and girls. Awkward attempts at climbing, skipping, hopping, and playing catch. Activities should utilize large muscles of the body.	Uses common words freely. Relates events in time order. Little concept of geographic relationships. Forms triangle from square piece of paper. Draws in some detail; likes to copy letters and numbers. Pragmatist rather than imaginative.	Great talker, 2000 word vocabulary. Goes about neighborhood unattended. Lives in world of here and now. Wants small responsibilities; readily asks for help. Developing sense of humor. Begins to fit into culture. Self interest quite strong. Play is still main business. Loves repetition. In wrong doing, commonly blames someone else. Doesn't connect death to himself or people he knows. Wants to know why people don't fall out of heaven. Questions are very concrete and specific.
6 years Grade 1	Body proportions close to those of an adult. Muscles beginning to develop faster than rest of body. 90% of adult brain weight achieved. Variety of physical skills. Climbs agilely. Can hop, skip, jump, and gallop. Can bounce a ball,	Learns by participation rather than rote. Dogmatic. Has difficulty in making decisions. Realistic view of death. Vivid imagination. Prints simple words. Tells what part of a picture is missing. Short attention span. Music reading	Likes parties, some social routines. Expresses aggression verbally. Self-interest, bossy, wants own way. Vivid imagination. Enjoys Bible stories and Sunday School. Prayer and relatedness to God important. Susceptible to teach-

*Compiled by Mary Lou McBroom, Lois Beck, and Edgar M. Turrentine.

Development Chart of Children 5-17 (Continued)

Age	Physical	Mental	Social-Emotional
	play catch, ride a tricycle, roller skate, and jump rope.	readiness. Readiness for reading comes at a mental age of 6½.	ings about the devil. Fears mother may die. Beginning to have an interest in the past.
7 years Grade 2	Heart and lungs smaller in relation to rest of body than at any other time of life. Graceful, speedy, agile. Able to master complicated dance steps.	Points out similarities; wood, coal, etc. Short attention span. A good listener. Seems more introverted and reflective. Mental life embracing community and cosmos. Attaining orientation in time and space.	Uses table knife for spreading butter. Beginning of ethical sense. Standardizes own behavior, judges others. Honesty begins to develop, but is sometimes overpowered by wants. Less lying. Time is conceived in terms of schedules. Death more personalized. Begins to understand that there are powers beyond himself over which he has no control. May laugh at or criticize self.
8 years Grade 3	Has acquired 12 of his permanent teeth. Can perform motor skills such as hopping, jumping, skipping, and bouncing a ball with a certain amount of grace. Average girl a year ahead of average boy in bone development. Body movements fluid, graceful, and poised.	Tells time to quarter of an hour. Remembers details from a story. Masters new words from contexts, prefixes, and syllables. Uses table of contents and index in a book. Prefers a cue or hint rather than direct orders. More expansive intellectually. Can	Talkative, interrupts. Likes to do things in a certain, preferably familiar, order. More responsible for acts; blames self, apologizes. Some concepts of good and bad from peers as well as parents. Likes to acquire, own, barter; gloats over his possessions; is money

Development Chart of Children 5-17 (Continued)

Age	Physical	Mental	Social-Emotional
		distinguish fundamental differences and similarities.	mad. Is expansive, but distinguishes fact from fancy. Perplexed about life after death. Not clear about placing events and people in history. Adventurous. Uses code language. Becoming vividly aware of sex differences.
9 years Grade 4	An optimal age for perfecting proficiency in tool subjects. Constantly improving co-ordination and capacity to learn physical skills.	Reads on own initiative. Copies designs from memory. Interested in facts and details. Power of self appraisal. Gives outward appearance of absent-mindedness. Fond of making inventories; likes to classify and identify; has a factual interest in seriations and categories.	Doesn't like interruptions. Is very busy. Relatively well organized. Likes to plan in advance and see ahead. Likes order; classifies and identifies information. Only feebly motivated by money. Likes to be trusted; is dependable and responsible. Is a realist; lack of interest in God; no longer believes in Santa Claus and fairy tales. Each sex cordially disdains the other.
10 years Grade 5	Gains made in musculature, but muscle fatigue still appears more rapidly than in healthy adults. Is more capable of	Repeats six digits. Difference between individuals becoming more pronounced. Time is related to happenings, whether	Makes minor purchases. Makes telephone calls. Most important virtue in friend is trust. Strict moral concern for self and

Development Chart of Children 5-17 (Continued)

Age	Physical	Mental	Social-Emotional
	little courteous amenities that have a motor basis. Girls' biological growth equal to that of a 12-year-old boy. Growth is proportionately less rapid than during primary years.	he is late or early for something. Talents now declare themselves. Thinks of God as a partner to make him a better person; offers self-made prayers.	peers. Truthful; avoids lying by silence. Judges cheating and swearing as awful. Doesn't like drunkenness. Sex differences are pronounced; girls have more poise, more folk wisdom, and more interest in matters pertaining to marriage and family. Receptive to social information, broadening ideas, prejudices, and liberalizing ideas. Girls more aware of inter-personal relationships.
11 years Grade 6	Eats incessantly. Possesses 20 of the 32 permanent teeth. Girls have overtaken boys in both stature and weight. Girls have entered the phase of rapid growth preceding puberty.	20% have reached adolescence. Does wide range of reading including comics. Repeats sentence from memory (15 to 16 words). Does not listen to reason.	A time of turmoil. Transition from the individualistic period to the gang age. Realizes when he does things wrong. Rejects what is expected of him. Talkative: endless detail. Hypercritical of self and others, but resentful of others' criticism. Well developed sense of ethics. Depends on alibies. Girls take blame better than boys. Girls run in cliques; emotional intense, and involved relationships. Boys form friendships

Development Chart of Children 5-17 (Continued)

Age	Physical	Mental	Social-Emotional
			with one or two, but mostly gangs. Some girls not interested in boys. Boys are neutral. Sometimes boys and girls are interested in each other.
12 years Grade 7	Sexual "coming of age." Glandular development and sex-related contour. Boys' pubescent spurt begins: Shoulders broaden, chest cavity increases, voice changes, develops coloration of facial hair. Full development of sex drive in males; partial development in girls. Brain and nervous system physically mature.	40% are adolescent. Understands abstract words.	Warm, bubbling, uninhibited. Enjoys group activity. Generally well-adjusted behavior. Separation of sexes in play. Interest in clubs. Enthusiasm for teams. Cooperation is learned. Boy's idea of a happy person is a noisy, raucous type. Girls consider prim, ladylike standards.
13 years Grade 8	Girl has achieved 95% growth. Boys start to grow sharply. Hands and feet have reached adult size: natural awkwardness.	60% adolescents. Worries a lot, especially about popularity, money, schoolwork. Firm conscience. Unscrambles a sentence.	Reflective, withdrawn. Peer groups are most important: center of youth's experience with personal identity and stability. Peer groups' opinions are agreed to before parents' opinions. Think of themselves as children. Sense of individuality. Self-criticism and independent capacity is at fresh peak. Desire independence. Begins to establish a sense of

Development Chart of Children 5-17 (Continued)

Age	Physical	Mental	Social-Emotional
			identity: who he is and his role in society.
14 years Grade 9	Few boys may shave periodically. Boys grow faster and voice deepens. Boys are again taller than girls. Peak of physical skills for girls.	80% adolescents. Solves oral problems of determined difficulty.	Happy, outgoing, expansive. Girls like boys, boys like girls. Clothes conscious: neat. Gets along better with teacher. Boisterousness and showing off considered childish. Girls shift from conformity to being a good sport.
15 years Grade 10	Girl's figure is womanly. Boy's body is so large his head seems smaller proportionately.	Begins to follow current events. Boys concentrate better than girls. A complex, bewildering age.	Spirit of independence. Generally, quiet, thoughtful. Gets along with father better than mother. Interests not so broad. Dating. Would rather be alone than with family.
16 years Grade 11	Boys reach 98% growth: increased musculature, equals the adult proportion.	Full of self-assurance. Doesn't worry needlessly.	Lot of dating. Good sense of humor. Friends are extremely important. Girls are marriage-minded, boys are not.
17 years Grade 12	Youth has just about gained proportions characteristic of adulthood. Females decline in physical endurance: now equals that of a 6 or 8 year old.		Brains minus social skills are not admired. Popularity for boys achieved by appearance, easy social manners, and smooth social dancing. Girls must be stylish.

Perception and Music

Again turning to *Webster's Collegiate Dictionary*, to perceive is "to obtain knowledge through the senses." Perception is the "direct acquaintance with anything through the senses" and "an immediate or intuitive cognition or judgment, often implying nice observation or subtle discrimination." It is an act comprised of apprehension and comprehension. In other words, it is the ability to receive an external impression and, then, to give, interpret, or understand the meaning of the external impression. Since music is an aural art, the music teacher is concerned, primarily, with refining the student's aural sense, but he also is concerned with developing the ability to give, interpret, or understand the meaning of what the ear hears. If the student is actually to experience music (compose, perform), as distinguished from vicariously experiencing music (listening), he must be taught the symbolism of the sounds he hears, which involves a visual training, and to reproduce, physically, from the symbolism, the sounds, which involves the motor aspect. Some of the distinctions in intuitive cognition or judgment with which the teacher is concerned in refining, whether they be aural, visual, or motor, are:

high — low	duple — triple
loud — soft	consonance — dissonance
pure — rich	repose — movement
fast — slow	like — unlike
strong — weak	antecedent — consequent
long — short	balance — imbalance

It is his concern to develop, from the gross to the fine, the ability to make these distinctions. The degree of fineness may be a measure of musical perception.

Aural

In his research on musical ability, Seashore stated:

> The ear is probably as sensitive to sound in the first year of childhood as it ever will be thereafter. The change that takes place with maturation and education consists of the development of the ability to assign meaning, develop habits of selection, and give accurate account of it.[1]

In describing what the ear can do, Seashore pointed out the following facts:

> The lower limit of hearing is about 16 cycles, the upper limit is about 16,000 cycles, and an extremely sensitive ear may hear up to 25,000 cycles.
> The just-noticeable-difference in pitch is about .06 of a whole tone in the average listener and .01 of whole tone in the sensitive listener.
> The average listener hears about 1,400 steps of difference in pitch.
> The minimum duration necessary in order to identify the pitch of a tone is from .04 to .09 of a second.
> The upper limit of loudness which the ear can tolerate is about 125 decibels.
> A very fine musical ear may detect a difference in the length of two notes as small as .01 second.[2]

Starting with these facts of physical ability to hear, the teacher must then devise a means to refine these physical abilities through practice and to guide the student in giving meaning to what he hears. For example, in cultivating the ability to make distinctions between high and low one can deduce that the starting interval is that which the teacher uses in the very first singing "tone games." Whether the particular interval is the most efficient one with which to begin may be only a matter of conjecture, for there has been very little research on the matter. How fine a distinction a child can make when he embarks on his formal education is partly due to his preschool experiences, but the question can be raised whether current music teaching procedures capitalize on these preschool experiences. Many teaching procedures, among them the Carl Orff *Music for Children*, start the refining process with

---

[1]Carl E. Seashore, *Psychology of Music* (McGraw-Hill Book Co., Inc., 1938), p. 79.
[2]*Ibid.*

the falling minor third — a pitch difference of 135 cycles! Compare this to Seashore's statement that the average ear can distinguish a difference in pitch of about three cycles. This is, of course, an over simplification of the matter. It is not only a physical difference in pitch, but a process of giving meaning to the two pitches — relating the pitches — which is being developed. The question then arises as to what are the desired meanings, the desired relationships, and are these valid? They are valid insofar as they are a part of the "set of tonal relations which serve as a tonal reference and pass judgment upon all tonal material as permissable or not permissable for musical usage" in a given culture.[3] (There has been much discussion recently whether current elementary school music teaching procedures are perpetuating a nineteenth century, romantic aesthetic. If so, is this valid?)

Another example: is there any relationship of the refinement of the distinction between fast and slow, strong and weak, long and short, to motor (muscle) refinement? It would seem there is a positive one. Can the child make a real distinction between fast and slow, strong and weak, long and short unless he possesses the maturation of motor development to feel, physically, the fastness and slowness, strongness and weakness, longness and shortness? Such distinctions must be experienced grossly — by the large body muscles — before they can be experienced finely by the mind's "ear." It is common knowledge that a child's understanding of past, present, and future is a developing process. It would seem also that to give meaning, interpretation, and understanding to the fine distinctions of time in music one must be able to understand the fine distinctions of past, present, and future in his other activities. To experience vicariously, one must have actually experienced. The meaning, interpretation, and understanding the ear gives to what it apprehends, therefore, is dependent upon what has been experienced. Perhaps the reason music teachers enjoy less success in teaching rhythm than is desirable is because there has been so little research in this area of musical behavior.

Visual

Too often music teaching is concerned only with the symbolism of music and not music itself. The visual is emphasized to the exclusion of the aural. Again it should be stated emphatically: music is an aural art.

---

[3]Assan D. Kresteff, "The Growth of Musical Awareness in Children," *Bulletin* No. 1, 1963 (Council for Research in Music Education), p. 5. This article is a report of a learning sequence of pitch relationships which is based on tonic-dominant harmony.

Symbolism makes it possible for one to experience richly — to partake of the experience of others separated from him, temporally and spatially. Musical symbolism is merely a representation of aural experiences. However, for one's actual experiences in the aural art to be passed on to and experienced by another there must be a common symbolism established. For a symbol to have meaning the experience which it represents must have been experienced by those employing the symbol. This is the teacher's job, to present the experience and its symbol so that the student may draw upon this, in the future, in order to give meaning, interpretation, and understanding to his contacts with music.

Much has been written, discussed, and argued about the different methods of presenting symbolism. Pitch symbolism has been presented with as much success as failure by means of syllables, numbers, and letter-names. So, too, has there been much pedagogical to-do about French time syllables, number-counting systems, mnemonic devices, and action words in teaching the symbolism of rhythm. What there has not been is enough research on the actual visual sense and its apprehension and comprehension of the symbols. What little research there has been has not been disseminated enough for any widespread practical application of its findings.

L. K. Bean attempted to determine the complexity of the musical pattern which can be perceived at one fixation of the eyes. He also attempted to show the effects of practice with a tachistoscope on the visual perception span. His study indicated that efficient readers are able to see four, five, or more symbols at a fixation. Inefficient or slow readers are only able to see one or two symbols at a fixation. He classified music readers into two groups: (1) the pattern-reader who reads groups of notes and (2) the part-reader who reads only one or two notes at a time. Practice with a tachistoscope indicated that part-readers could become pattern-readers, in other words, the visual perceptive span could be increased.[4] Such a Gestalt approach to music reading should alert the music teacher to factors other than methods of teaching involved in the learning process.

In another experiment, the same researcher investigated the use of visual, auditory, and kinesthetic imagery in the transfer of musical notation to the piano keyboard. He found that almost all of the subjects in his experiment capitalized most on visual imagery.

Hutton compared two methods of developing sight-singing ability, one using audio-visual aids and the other not. In the same investigation she attempted to determine the relationship between verbal reading

---

[4]L. K. Bean, "An Experimental Approach to the Reading of Music," *Psychological Monographs*, Vol. 50, No. 6 (1938).

ability and music reading ability. She concluded from her research that audio-visual aids had a more beneficial effect on the teaching of sight-singing to her fourth grade students. She also reported there was no significant correlation between music reading ability and verbal reading ability.[5]

Several researchers have studied the relationship of eye movement to music reading. One of these, O. I. Jacobsen, has reported an interesting investigation. He attempted to determine the characteristics of the eye movement of readers at various stages of accomplishment in music reading. He also attempted to determine the type of development taking place in the learning process of music reading. Some of his conclusions were: mere training of eye movement does not lead to a more efficient reading of the music score; flash cards seemed to be a more efficient manner of improving music reading; the most accurate readers were also the fastest readers.[6] Lannert and Ullman concluded, after investigating the reading of piano music, that the ability to "read ahead," the number of eye movements from the notation to the keyboard, and the ability to read ledger lines were determinants of this proficiency.[7] Ortmann, investigating the reading of chords found: the more notes in a chord, the greater the chance for error; the greater the vertical distance between the top and bottom note, the greater the chance for error; and, the eyes tends to give more attention to those notes grouped more closely together than the extremes in a chord.[8] He also found, in another investigation, that chord groups and melodic groups can be read as units in a time which, for all musical purposes, can be considered instantaneous and that normal note-reading problems are not due to actual eye difficulties, but rather to an inability to group the distribution of notes into larger perceptual units. He concluded that problems in reading, such as the number of notes in the field, the area covered by the distribution of these notes, the number of linear dimensions involved, complexity or symmetry of note patterns, and the meaning of the note group from either a harmonic or melodic standpoint, or both, appear to be the major causes of difficulty in sight-reading.[9]

---

[5]Doris Hutton, "A Comparative Study of Two Methods of Training Sight-Singing in the Fourth Grade," *Journal of Research in Music Education,* 1 (1953), pp. 119-126.

[6]O. I. Jacobsen, "An Analytic Study of Eye-Movements in Reading Vocal and Instrumental Music," *Journal of Musicology,* 3 (1941), pp. 197-226.

[7]V. Lannert and M. Ullman, "Factors in the Reading of Piano Music," *American Journal of Psychology,* 58 (1945) pp. 91-9.

[8]O. Ortmann, "The Elements of Chord Reading in Music Notation," *Journal of Experimental Education,* 3 (1934).

[9]————, "Span of Vision in Note Reading," *Music Educators National Conference Journal,* 23 (1937), pp. 88-93.

King, after a study of certain aspects of aural and visual abilities as they relate to music reading, concluded, rather discouragingly, that the knowledge of music symbols has little direct relationship to the ability to use these symbols for obtaining correct musical expressions.[10] In another investigation he found a significant relationship between intelligence, as determined by I.Q. tests, and the ability to read music.[11]

If the writers were to make a recommendation it would be that music teachers should make a more concerted effort to explore, capitalize on, and apply the research findings of the verbal reading specialists to their own subject. Surely, the problems of coping with one type of symbolism are very little different than those of another, also, the visual sense perception problems of the one are very little different than those of the other.

Motor

It has been hinted, in a preceding paragraph, that motor development plays an important role in musical accomplishment. Much is known about human motor development, but much less is known about the upper limits of the abilities dependent on motor development. What man is physically capable of doing has still to be determined. The *Developmental Chart* in the preceding section gives one an approximate idea of the physical development of the human being. The following summarizes that chart and serves as a reminder, again, of the different stages of physical growth.

MAJOR AGE-PERIODS IN PHYSICAL GROWTH

Period	Boys	Girls
1. Infancy	Birth – 1 year	Birth – 1 year
Newborn	1st 2 weeks	1st 2 weeks
Infancy	up to 1 year	up to 1 year
2. Childhood	1-16 years	1-15 years
Early	1-6 years	1-6 years
Mid	6 to 9-10 years	6 to 9-10 years
Late	9-10 to 13-16 years	9-10 to 12-15 years
3. Puberty	13-14 years	12-13 years
4. Adolescence	13-14 to 18-20 years	12-13 to 18-20 years
5. Adulthood	18-20 years plus	18-20 years plus[12]

---

[10]Harry A. King, "Auditory and Visual Characteristics of Poor Music Readers," *Music Educators National Conference Yearbook* (1939-40).
[11]————, "A Study of Relationship of Music Reading and I. Q. Scores," *Journal of Research in Music Education*, II/1 (Spring, 1954).
[12]*Physical Growth* (The Philadelphia Center for Research in Child Growth, n. d.), p. 9.

Motor development, in its psychological sense, refers to muscular movement or manipulation. The assumption that physical development is the same as motor development is an erroneous one. Motor development may be a result of practice, physical development is not. Motor development, through practice, is dependent upon physical maturation, but motor development as a result of physical maturation does not necessarily follow. A task involving a muscle dexterity is dependent on that muscle's maturity to absorb the practice necessary for the dexterity. Too often, music teachers call upon their students for a muscle dexterity which is not warranted because of the student's physical immaturity.

Motor development progresses from the more generalized movement or manipulation to the specialized, and from the specialized movement or manipulation to inclusive movements or manipulations which correlate actions which in the earlier stages were practiced separately. Children who are either slow or fast in the initial stages of motor development tend to maintain that rate of development. Children who tend to be highly competent in one motor activity tend to be highly competent in other motor activities, however, this holds more truth for those activities involving large muscles than for those activities involving the small muscles. There is a positive relationship, albeit low, between mental and motor ability and achievement. Providing children with equipment and opportunities is conducive to motor development. Children in competition with other children tend to develop dexterity more quickly. Also, instruction geared to the child's level will be an aid to motor development. Encouragement from adults also helps.

Carried to the extreme, provision of equipment, competition, instruction, and encouragement may serve only to frustrate rather than to hasten motor development. There must be an accompanying physical maturation for these factors to serve positively. In the section on PHYSICAL DEVELOPMENT it has already been pointed out, "in the learning of complex skills or other accomplishments requiring training, that practice is most effective at the point of maturation — not before, but also, not long after the period of physical readiness." Also, "encouraging children, before the age of physical readiness, may actually retard the development of the skill by impairing the desire and eagerness for learning the skill."

The problem facing the music teacher, or any teacher for that matter, is in determining when the physical-mental-social-emotional readiness occurs for the learning of a certain skill involving motor dexterity. The Philadelphia Center for Research in Child Growth defines this physical readiness as "maturation age," as apart from chronological and mental age. Even if music teachers could pinpoint more accurately the stages of physical development — maturation age — it would be a long step towards the improved efficiency in developing the motor skills requisite to their art. The Philadelphia Center points out that the bone structure of the hand provides a most efficient measure of maturation age.[13] If there was an application of this criterion to the development of musical motor skills, improved efficiency in teaching (and learning) would result. For example, the time for starting children on musical instrument performance might be established more efficiently than it is now. The time is now the fourth, fifth, or sixth grade level, being based more or less on a chronological age, irrespective of sex, when it is an established fact that girls, at this time, are already from one to two years ahead of boys in physical maturation.

Another criterion for determining motor development, which has not been explored as thoroughly as it should be, is the motility test developed and standardized by Ream.[14] (Motility is the capability of spontaneous movement.) Ream's test is based on finger-tapping. However, to be completely practical, the movement being subjected to testing should be the same, or almost the same, as that demanded by the skill for which one is seeking knowledge. Although the results of this type of test can be improved with practice, it does have predictive value if chronological and mental age are considered.

The music teacher may wonder why the above discussion on motor development should be included under the heading of PERCEPTION. He should remind himself that much of the motor development demanded in music depends on the highly developed sense of touch and feel as governed by the aural and visual senses. Hence, the music teacher, availing himself of the knowledge of all the aspects of human development, will be much better equipped to guide the student toward a more complete experiencing of music.

Imagery

Almost all of the research related to musical perception has been more concerned with such topics as "imagery," "musical meaning," "expression in music," and "ideational content" than with sense perception. Some of these terms have dual meanings — imagery, for example. In a

---

[13]*Ibid.*, p. 12. Also, see: Greulich, W. W. and S. I. Pyle. *Radiographic Atlas of Skeletal Development of the Hand and Wrist*, 2nd ed. Palo Alto: Stanford University Press, 1959.

[14]M. J. Ream, *The Tapping Test — A Measure of Motility* (University of Iowa Studies in Psychology, VIII-1922).

number of musical tests it means the matching of a visual symbol with an aural one. The other meaning concerns the power to evoke extra-musical meanings. Extra-musical perception has been the subject for much serious debate. The debate revolves around the manner in which a person should listen to music. Some think one should listen only for the intrinsic beauty with no extra-musical ideas intruding upon the listening process. Others think music can, and should convey extra-musical ideas.

Among the first to investigate musical expressiveness, scientifically, was Gilman, in 1892. In an experiment he compared his reactions to a musical composition with those of twenty other persons. He found little agreement of reactions.[15] Downey, a few years later, after an experiment involving the reception of impressions from music, concluded that great differences existed between individuals to receive definite impressions from music.[16] Weld, reporting in the same journal a number of years later, after an experiment, concluded that music, by itself, cannot tell a detailed story with any degree of accuracy.[17] On the other hand, Helmholtz, after an acoustical study, reported that types of music can convey general impressions, for instance, the brilliant and pentrating tone quality of brass instruments is well-suited to giving the impression of power.[18] Valentine also reported a commonality of impressions to musical intervals, however, he found there was some disagreement.[19]

Schoen, after experimentation, concluded there was a marked consistency in the mood response which music arouses.[20] Barrett, in agreement with Schoen, reported, after investigation, that "musical meaning" tends to remain constant and variances occur in proportion to the ability to perceive that meaning.[21] After experimenting, Heinlein stated that the major and minor quality of a chord has a certain amount of affective meaning, probably due to training.[22]

[15]Benjamin I. Gilman, "Report on an Experimental Test of Musical Expressiveness," *American Journal of Psychology*, IV (1892), pp. 558-76.

[16]June E. Downey, "A Musical Experiment," *American Journal of Psychology*, IX (1897), pp. 63-9.

[17]H. P. Weld, "An Experimental Study of Musical Enjoyment," *American Journal of Psychology*, XXIII (1912), pp. 245-308.

[18]H. L. Helmholtz, *On the Sensations of Tone as a Physiological Basis for the Theory of Music*, 4th ed. (New York: Longmans, Green Inc., 1912), pp. 118-19.

[19]C. W. Valentine, "The Aesthetic Appreciation of Musical Intervals Among School Children and Adults," *British Journal of Psychology*, VI (1913), pp. 190-216.

[20]Max Schoen, *The Effects of Music* (New York: Harcourt, Brace, and Co., Inc., 1927), pp. 150-71.

[21]Roger L. Barrett, *The Study of the General Nature of Ideational Perception: Music* (unpublished doctoral dissertation, University of Iowa, 1961 — *Dissertation Abstracts*, XXII/8/2814), p. 18.

[22]C. P. Heinlein, "The Affective Character of the Major and Minor Modes in Music," *Journal of Comparative Psychology*, VIII (1928), pp. 101-42.

Gundlach investigated the various characteristics within music which cause expressive meanings to be assigned to music. He found that speed and rhythm, in that order, were the important characteristics and melodic range was of least importance.[23] Ortmann, seemingly in contradiction, reported tonal intensity as the basis of the more complex reactions to music.[24] However, Hevner, disagreeing with both Gundlach and Ortmann, reported that meaning in music is dependent on the listener.[25] Later, she reported pitch and tempo were also important determinants of the affective quality of music.[26]

Rigg, experimenting with college students, reported that these college students agreed upon the joyfulness or sadness of music, but when finer discriminations were demanded there was less agreement.[27] Barrett took exception to this experiment because he thought joyfulness and sadness were associated with tempo and the performance of the same music by different conductors would vary enough in tempo so that one could not attach such affective meanings to a composition.[28]

From the above reports, one can say that music does convey an extra-musical meaning to the listener. However, the extra-musical meaning does not possess any commonality except in the most general terms. A specific musical composition, if it does have extra-musical meaning, possesses it only because society has assigned it that meaning. Here, again, the teacher's task is to develop the student's sense perception so that he can apprehend and comprehend the meanings, interpretations, and understandings society has assigned to the music.

---

[23]Ralph Gundlach, "Factors Determining the Characterization of Musical Phrases," *American Journal of Psychology*, XLVII (1935), pp. 624-44.

[24]O. Ortmann, "Tonal Intensity as an Aesthetic Factor," *Musical Quarterly*, XIV (1928), pp. 178-91.

[25]Kate Hevner, "The Affective Character of the Major and Minor Modes in Music," *American Journal of Psychology*, XLVII (1935), pp. 103-18.

[26]————, "The Affective Value of Pitch and Tempo in Music," *American Journal of Psychology*, XLIX (1937), pp. 621-30.

[27]Melvin Rigg, "An Experiment to Determine How Accurately College Students Can Interpret the Intended Meanings of Musical Compositions," *Journal of Experimental Psychology*, XXI (1937), pp. 223-29.

[28]Barrett, *op. cit.*, p. 25.

Learning Theory and Music

How, and when does learning take place? Upon the answer to this question depends a theory of learning. As to so many other questions concerning man, there have been many answers proferred to this one. If one has an answer, he then has a deeper insight into how to teach.

Significant Learning Theories

The Platonic and Aristotelian concepts of the deductive mode of thought with its syllogistic method held sway over all formal teaching in the Western world for centuries. Francis Bacon (1521-1626) questioned this method and suggested in its place a scientific approach. In his *Novum Organum* he propounded an inductive mode of thought. He believed truth came from the observation of, and experience in nature. In other words, truth was a result of man's reasoning, based on his observing and experiencing nature. Hence, man learned through observation (empiricism) — through the experience gained through his five senses (sense realism). Johann Comenius (1592-1670) carried on this line of reasoning. He explained in *The Great Didactic* that teaching is a science. Education is a step-by-step process of the development of sense-perception. John Locke (1632-1704), through his *Some Thoughts Concerning Education*, further developed the concept of sense-realism. He believed that, at birth, the mind is a "clean slate" (*tabula rasa*), ready to perceive, through the senses, impressions of the environment. Ideas, he thought, were not already in the mind waiting for expression, but were a result of sense-perception of the environment. Jean Jacques

71

Rousseau (1712-1778) was the great popularizer of the concept of sense-realism. He conceived thinking man as being a product of his experience within his environment, thus, education should be based upon the direct experiencing and observation of the environment (nature) rather than the vicarious experiencing through books. Rousseau's educational theories were rather haphazardly stated in his two books, *Émile* and *La Nouvelle Heloise.*

Just as Rousseau was the populizer of sense-realism, Johann Pestalozzi (1746-1827) was the leading interpreter of the theory. He developed a series of "object lessons" by which the senses could be trained systematically. In other words, man learns by doing. In the United States, Joseph Neef (1770-1854) and William Maclure (1763-1840) pioneered Pestalozzianism and Edward A. Sheldon (1823-1897), at the Oswego State Normal School, popularized Pestalozzianism. Of interest to the music teacher is that Hans Georg Nägeli (1773-1836) worked with Pestalozzi in applying Pestalozzi's principles to music teaching. Also of interest to the music teacher is that Elam Ives (and, perhaps, Lowell Mason) pioneered the application of Pestalozzi's and Nägeli's principles of teaching music in the United States.[1]

Friedrich Froebel (1782-1852), following in the sense-realism footsteps of Pestalozzi, felt the educative process should start much earlier in life — with the three- and four-year old. As explained in his *Education of Man,* the education of the young should be activity centered rather than book centered. Out of this belief grew the kindergarten movement. Its first appearance in the United States, in 1855, in Watertown, Wisconsin, was through the initiative of Mrs. Schurz, the wife of one of President Lincoln's advisors.

Another German philosopher contributing greatly to the "how and when" of teaching was Johann Herbart (1776-1841). Herbart's thesis was that history and literature served as the core around which all the other subjects should be correlated and concentrated, or associated (theory of associationism). The theory of associationism was developed in his *Outline of Educational Doctrine.* Out of this concept of association came his Five Formal Steps of teaching: (1) preparation, (2) presentation, (3) association, (4) generalization, and (5) application. His "theory of recapitulation" received widespread interest and continues to

---

[1]For interesting discussions concerning the implied controversy, see: Ellis, Howard E. "Lowell Mason and the *Manual of the Boston Academy of Music." Journal of Research in Music Education,* III (Spring, 1955); and, John, Robert W. "Elam Ives and the Pestalozzian Philosophy of Education." *Journal of Research in Music Education,* VIII (Spring, 1960). For a complete account of Pestalozzianism in music, see: Ellis, Howard E. *The Influence of Pestalozzianism on Instruction in Music.* Unpublished doctoral dissertation, University of Michigan, 1957.

crop up in educational circles. The "theory" holds that a child is born into this world in a primitive state and that he must be led through the various stages of man's development from the prehistoric primitive state to his present high level of social, cultural, political, and moral development. This task is primarily the responsibility of the formal educational institution.

With the appearance of Darwin's *Origin of the Species* in 1859, a completely new and different idea of man and his environment enveloped the intellectual world. Serving as one of the interpreters of this new idea to the area of education was Herbert Spencer (1820-1903), an Englishman. In his *Education: Intellectual, Moral, and Physical* he took the scientific viewpoint that man and his environment are ever changing and, hence, the education of man should follow the scientific in order for him to cope with this constant changing. This type of education is of "most worth" Spencer concluded.

From the stress on the scientific examination of man and his environment developed such research as Max Wundt's sense-perception research, Alfred Binet's intelligence testing, Ivan Pavlov's study of conditioned reflexes, and Francis Galton's genetic studies. Out of this and other great quantities of research developed E. L. Thorndike's theory of stimulus-response (S-R psychology). From his theory of stimulus-response, he developed his laws of learning: the law of exercise, the law of effect, and the law of belonging, which were elaborately defined in his multi-volume *Educational Psychology*. Thorndike finally concluded that man's accomplishments were more a product of nature rather than nurture.

In contrast to Thorndike's "school" of objective psychology (besides Thorndike, Lewis Terman, G. Stanley Hall, James Cattell, Joseph Jastrow, and others) which stressed the scientific methods of the study of man, a group of scholars, namely, George H. Mead, Charles Peirce, William James, and culminating with the work of John Dewey, expressed a social concept of man. Man is a social being, shaped by social forces, and becomes an individual because he "finds" himself in the social context. Truth, they held, is a result of experience in the social context and it changes as the social context changes. This concept of truth is the root of the pragmatic philosophy. John Dewey (1859-1951) related this philosophy to the educational endeavor. He propounded the view that education was a social process, a process which shaped the student. It is a process which re-creates the past experiences of a society for the student; in other words, it is a process of experiencing (experimentalism). Education is living and not a preparation for living. The search for truth is a testing of ideas. In his *How We Think* he elaborated on how an idea is tested; from this came his five-step process of thinking (PART III, INTRODUCTION). Dewey, more than any other man, influenced American education, thus far, in the twentieth century.

The argument between nature and nurture grew more intense shortly after the first World War. From the work of John B. Watson and others, based on Pavlov's experiments in conditioning, came the viewpoint that behavior is a product of conditioning. Hence, education is a process of presenting the necessary stimuli in order to elicit the desired response (behaviorist psychology). Carried to the ultimate, one must conclude that everyone, at birth, has the same potential behavior if subjected to the same stimuli. From Germany came the idea that learning is not a result of responding to specifics, but is a result of a consideration of the whole (Gestalt psychology). Another theory of learning holds that man's behavior is a result of his reactions to psychological forces, therefore learning will take place if goals with psychological rewards are placed before the learner (topological psychology).

Current Learning Theory

Butts and Cremin,[2] in a recent book, listed four issues confronting twentieth-century educational endeavors. One of these is "the nature of the educational program in the schools and colleges," in other words, how, when, and what to teach. During the late fifties and the early sixties the educational pendulum swung towards the scientific. It now appears to be swinging back, not without, however, acquiring certain scientific characteristics. Because it is too close in time to make any valid evaluations or predictions, one can only report some of the more significant developments.

Out of a conference held in 1959[3] — its purpose was "to examine the fundamental processes involved in imparting to young students a sense of the substance and method of science"[4] — emerged an individual who is articulating, with some degree of popularity, an approach to teaching. Such catch phrases as his "structured learning," "spiral curriculum," and "economy of teaching" have quickly become part of the professional jargon. The substance of his *The Process of Education* can be summarized by the following three statements:[5]

---

[2]R. Freeman Butts and Lawrence A. Cremin, *A History of Education in American Culture* (New York: Henry Holt and Co., 1953), p. 516.
[3]Woods Hole Conference, Cape Cod, Mass., in September, 1959.
[4]Jerome S. Bruner, *The Process of Education* (Cambridge: Harvard University Press, 1965), p. vii.
[5]*Ibid.*, pp. 9, 33, and 48.

We may take as perhaps the most general objective of education that it cultivates excellence . . .

. . . any subject can be taught effectively in some intellectually honest form to any child at any stage of development.

Learning a subject seems to involve three almost simultaneous processes . . . acquisition . . . transformation . . . evaluation . . .

(It is interesting to compare his three-fold process of the "act of learning" with Herbart's Five Formal Steps, or Dewey's "complete act of thought," or even Highet's "three stages of teaching."[6]) This man, Jerome S. Bruner of Harvard University, has based his concepts, in part, on those researched and developed by Jean Piaget in Geneva, Switzerland.

Jean Piaget, born in 1896 in Switzerland, director of the Psychology Laboratory at Geneva, has spent a lifetime of research on child development. Because almost all of the reports of his research first appeared in the French language his work is not as generally well-known as it should be.[7] Piaget, from his research, has divided the development of children into three stages. The first, from birth to about five years of age, is called the "sensory-motor" and "pre-operational" stage; the second, from about five to ten years of age, is the stage of "concrete operations"; and the third, from about ten to fourteen years, the "formal operations" stage. Following is a further definition of these three stages:

Sensory-motor and Pre-operational	The use of reflexes The first acquired adaptations and the primary circular reactions
Concrete operations	The secondary circular reactions and the procedures destined to make interesting sights last
	The coordination of the secondary schemata and their application to new situations
Formal operations	The tertiary circular reactions and the discovery of new means through the active experimentation
	The invention of new means through mental combination[8]

---

[6]Gilbert Highet, *The Art of Teaching* (New York: Vintage Books, 1959), p. 66.

[7]His works, now, are generally available in English translation. A most excellent summarization of his work is: Flavell, John H. *The Developmental Psychology of Jean Piaget* (The University Series in Psychology, David C. McClelland, editor). Princton: D. Van Nostrand Co., Inc., 1963.

[8]Jean Piaget, *The Origins of Intelligence in Children*, translated by Margaret Cook (New York: International Universities Press, Inc., 1952).

Concrete and formal operations have been defined in logico-mathematical formulas. Each formula represents a phase in the intellectual development of the child. For example, the concrete operations stage is divided into the manipulation of classes and relations of which the following formulas represent steps of progression in the development of the manipulation of classes:

$$A + A' = B \quad \text{Primary addition of}$$
$$\text{classes}$$
$$A + A' = A_2 + A'_2 \quad \text{Secondary addition of}$$
$$\text{classes}$$
$$A_1 + B_1 + C_1 = D_1 \quad \text{Bi-univocal multiplication}$$
$$\text{of classes[9]}$$

The problem for subject-matter specialists now becomes one of "structuring" their subject matter within the framework of these concrete and formal operations.

As mentioned above, the educational pendulum is swinging away from the extreme emphasis placed on the scientific, which was the characteristic for a few years in the fifties and sixties. Specifically, to what orientation it is swinging is largely conjecture. However, certain actions and events may be pointing to a specific orientation. Butts and Cremin cited the "control and support of education" as another of the four issues facing the educational establishment.[10] In the years since their writing, because of its increasing concern for the social welfare of its citizenry, the federal government has played an increasingly significant role in the "control and support of education." This, and a certain small (?) reaction to the extreme scientific orientation of the preceding years, has caused those concerned with education to return to the social theory of man as developed by Mead, Peirce, James, and Dewey. Such programs as the Peace Corps, Teaching Corps, Job Corps, VISTA, Operation Head-start, Upward Bound, Title One, and others seem to bear out this statement. The great foundational support of the arts and humanities which has developed in the sixties also seems to affirm this statement.

One most influential educator, James B. Conant, has listed the "democratic social component" as the first component of the four he deems necessary as the "intellectual equipment" required for developing

---

[9]Jean Piaget and Bärbel Inhelder, The Growth of Logical Thinking from Childhood to Adolescence, translated by Anne Parsons and Stanley Milgram (New York: Basic Books, Inc., 1958), chapter 17.

[10]R. Freeman Butts and Lawrence A. Cremin, op. cit.

the teaching skill.[11] He goes on to recommend: ". . . a teacher must know something about the processes by which social behavior emerges in groups of children."[12] These statements also seem to affirm that the educational endeavor is again becoming increasingly concerned with the social concept of man. One of the most articulate of the music sociologists also seems to affirm this concern with a social orientation when he writes of the "cultivated society" as being the ultimate "social order" for which society must strive. In his hierarchy of "social orders," it is interesting to note that his "cogno society," with its emphasis on "scientism," is just below his ideal social order, the "cultivated society."[13] In summary, one of the significant educational trends of the late sixties, and out of it a theory of learning, is:

> What the best and wisest parent wants for his own child, that must the community want for all of its children. Any other ideal for our schools is narrow and unlovely; acted upon, it destroys our democracy. All that society has accomplished for itself is put, through the agency of the school, at the disposal of its future members. All its better thoughts of itself it hopes to realize through the new possibilities thus opened to its future self. Here individualism and socialism are at one. Only by being true to the full growth of all the individuals who make it up, can society by any chance be true to itself.[14]

Application to Music Teaching

Research on how music learning is most efficiently accomplished is limited. In spite of the fact there has been a great increase in research on music and music teaching, it still is not possible to list any universal truisms concerning how music is learned. If any were to be offered, the theory of learning "by example and by precept" would be the one. In fact, if asked, the majority of music teachers would probably answer with "start where the student is and carry him as far as possible through example and by precept." The few significant and lasting innovations in music learning theory have, generally, been the result of the inventiveness and creativeness coming from the classroom rather than from controlled basic research. Actually, music teachers have followed the learning theory in vogue in the other subject-matter areas. In fact,

---

[11]James B. Conant, *The Education of American Teachers* (New York: McGraw-Hill Book Co., Inc., 1963), p. 113.

[12]*Ibid.*, p. 115.

[13]Max Kaplan, *Foundations and Frontiers of Music Education* (New York: Holt, Rinehart and Winston, Inc., 1966), p. 2.

[14]John Dewey, *The School and Society* (Chicago: University of Chicago Press, 1902), p. 7.

. . . many American music educators have demonstrated what may be considered an easy readiness to climb aboard any intellectual bandwagon which happened to be near by, and to trust it to arrive at destinations appropriate for music educators, or worse, to adopt its destinations as their own without careful scrutiny of the intellectual propriety involved.[15]

However, the influence of major learning theorists has affected the teaching of music.

As stated above, shortly after the turn of the century, with the stress on the scientific examination of man and his environment, much research was undertaken and accomplished. One research project, significant to music teaching, was that of Seashore. Out of his quest for defining music talent and the means to measure that talent, came a scientific approach to music teaching — that of the selection of music students. The Eastman School Experiment, undertaken under the direction of Hazel B. Stanton and with the encouragment of George Eastman and Howard Hanson, which was a practical application of Seashore's research, has had and continues to have an influence on the teaching of music in the United States.[16]

Herbart's "theory of recapitulation" has made at least two appearances on the music teaching scene, with some effect. The first application of the theory was by Satis N. Coleman. In the teaching of music to children she adopted the following theory:

> The natural evolution of music shall be my guide in leading the child from the simple to the complex, and we, with guidance, may probably often discover and cover in one lesson things that required generations for man, without guidance, to learn . . .[17]

Most recently, and receiving considerable attention, is Carl Orff's application of the "theory of recapitulation," in his *Music for Children,* to the teaching of music to children. Arnold Walter, in his Introduction to the English adaptation describes Orff's theory of learning (teaching) music, thusly:

---

[15]Allen P. Britton, "Music in Early American Public Education: A Historical Critique," *Basic Concepts in Music Education* (The Fifty-seventh Yearbook of the National Society for the Study of Education, Part I. Chicago: University of Chicago Press, 1958), p. 207.

[16]A brief account of the Eastman experiment is found in: Seashore, Carl E. "Analyses of Talent in a Music School." *Psychology of Music.* New York: McGraw-Hill Book Co., Inc., 1938. For a complete account see: Stanton, Hazel M. *Measurement of Musical Talent.* University of Iowa Studies in the Psychology of Music, II (1935).

[17]Satis N. Coleman, *Creative Music for Children* (New York: G. P. Putnam's Sons, 1928), p. 29.

. . . the growth of music must be re-enacted in a growing human being; that a child must be led through the various stages (from the most primitive to the more complex) which man traversed before music reached the level on which we find it now.[18]

An extension of Pestalozzian "object lessons" to the teaching of music might be the "experience charts" developed by Mary Helen Richards for her adaptation of the Kodaly system of music teaching.[19] How close an adaptation her system is to Kodaly's can be determined by examining the materials developed at the Third Street Music School Settlement, New York City[20] and to Percy Young's adaptation of Kodaly's *Choral Method*.[21]

Thorndike's S-R psychology has become increasingly popular in the last few years. This theory of learning is employed in the numerous music textbooks built on the "programmed instruction concept."

Behaviorist psychology, with its concept of conditioning, is the basis of still another theory of learning which is receiving much attention from instrumental music teachers. Shinichi Suzuki's violin method is based on the idea that children are conditioned by the environment to which they are exposed.

The publishers of the basic music textbook series have noted the theory of learning as interpreted by Bruner. Their use of the terms "structured learning" and "spiral curriculum" shows they are aware of this theory even though their textbooks may not be completely consistent with the theory. Marilyn Pflederer's attempts to apply Piaget's theories to music teaching are more noteworthy examples of the attempts to apply this theory.[22]

From the above examples, one can deduce there has been very little organized attack by the music teaching profession as a whole on how children learn music. If dramatic strides are to be made towards the "cultivated society" such an attack must soon be launched.

---

[18]Arnold Walter, "Introduction," *Music for Children*, adapted by Doreen Hall and Arnold Walter (New York: Associated Music Publishers, Inc., 1955), p. v.

[19]Mary Helen Richards, *Threshold to Music Program* (Palo Alto, Calif.: Fearon Publishers, Inc., 1966).

[20]Stephen Jay, Arpad Darazs, and Donald Stratton, unpublished materials.

[21]Zoltan Kodaly, *Choral Method*, adapted by Percy M. Young (New York: Boosey & Hawkes Music Publishers, Ltd., 1964), 15 vols.

[22]Marilyn Pflederer, *The Responses of Children to Musical Tasks Embodying Piaget's Principle of Conservation* (unpublished doctoral dissertation, University of Illinois, 1963 — *Dissertation Abstracts*, XXIV/11/4730); "How Children Conceptually Organize Musical Sounds," *Bulletin* No. 7, Spring, 1966 (Council for Research in Music Education).

Creativeness and Music

To create is to bring into being — to cause to exist. To imitate is to follow, copy, or reproduce. To originate is to give origin, to produce as new. Given these definitions, creating and originating may be synonymous, but originating and imitating are not. An act may be creative in the personal relation, but it may not be in the universal relation. Hence, creating and imitating may or may not also be synonymous. Thus, these definitions must be accepted subjectively rather than objectively.

To conform is to make like or be like. In other words, conforming is imitating. However, in the generally accepted sense, creating and conforming are antithetical. So, if education is the process, in part, of passing on the habits, customs, knowledge, skills, and techniques of a society to its younger members, which is a conforming process, how then can it also develop the capabilities of the younger members to maintain the progress of that society, which involves a creative process, when they take their places as adult members of the society? Must not the other part of education be the development of the capability to progress?

Society's definition of creativity is, very often, a too confining one. All persons are creative, some more than others. It is to these more creative individuals that the term is applied. An individual may solve a problem in a way which, to him, is unique, but to another individual may not be unique because the second individual functions at a higher level. When one recognizes the differences between individuals he then recognizes there are different levels of creativeness. That the existence of different levels of creativeness has been accepted slowly, can largely be attributed to the strength of the "great man" theory — the "genius" idea of the nineteenth century. This ideal, consciously or unconsciously, has been kept alive by the great rewards with which contemporary society has bestowed upon the superior creative talent. Although the "bolt-of-lightning-of-inspiration," "God-singled-out," "superbeing" concept of the creative person has been largely rejected in the twentieth century, there still is not agreement on what attributes constitute creativeness. There have been many investigations in the recent past attempting to isolate these attributes, but the results have been subjective and there has been no universal truth developed to guide teachers in the active development of this trait in their students.

The Institute of Personality Assessment and Research, University of California, categorizes the creative act into three types: (1) an expression of internally oriented pressures and needs; (2) an expression of externally oriented pressures and needs; and (3) an expression which is the product of external pressures and needs which lend themselves to solution by internal desires and goals. In defining the three types of the creative act it might be possible to infer from the definitions some attributes which may be necessary in order to function creatively. This organization, as well as other researchers, have also stated that intelligence, as measured by I.Q. tests, is not necessarily a measure of creative potential.[1] The attributes of creativeness might also be gleaned from another writer's description of the creative individual, an individual whom he describes as engaging in a continual process of self-renewal. He describes him as follows:

1. The self-renewing man is not imprisoned by fixed habits, attitudes and routines.
2. The self-renewing man never ceases to explore his own potentialities.
3. The self-renewing man will risk failure in order to learn.
4. The self-renewing individual respects the sources of his own energy and motivation.[2]

Yet another writer, in the same journal, has characterized the creative individual by listing his attributes:

a general openness to experience from both without and within; a toleration for ambiguity, confusion and disorder; the strong disposition

---

[1] Jackson and Getzels, from their research, concur with this.
[2] John W. Gardner, "You Can Tell a Creative Company by the People it Keeps," *Think* (International Business Machines Corp.), Vol. 28, No. 10 (Nov.-Dec., 1962), pp. 2-7.

to be independent rather than conforming; and the tendency to perceive through intuition rather than the senses.[3]

Given these characteristics of the creative individual, cannot the educational institution provide the necessary environment to nurture to full-flowering these characteristics within each student, each according to his own capability?

Intuitive Thinking

Almost all those involved in defining creativeness admit that the creative act is largely a problem-solving act. This problem-solving act possesses a certain uniqueness apart from the rational, sophisticated, elegant problem-solving method characteristic of the scientific method. Various writers have delineated the thought processes as involving intuitive thinking in one and analytical thinking in the other. Bruner defines the two types, thus:

> . . . intuitive thinking rests on familiarity with the domain of knowledge involved and with its structure, which makes it possible for the thinker to leap about, skipping steps and employing short cuts in a manner that requires a later rechecking of conclusions by more analytic means . . .
>
> Analytic thinking characteristically proceeds at a step at a time.[4]

It may be well to review the definitions of "intuitive" and "intuition." *Webster's Collegiate Dictionary* defines the one as "knowing or perceiving by intuition; having, or characterized by, intuition"; and the other as "immediate apprehension or cognition; the power of knowing or the knowledge obtained without recourse to inference or reasoning; insight; familiarly, a quick or ready apprehension."

One may infer from these definitions that, ideally, effective intuitive thinking is based on a complete experience with and knowledge of the subject about which the thinking revolves. At this point one may refer back to the statement about the different levels of experience and knowledge of a subject existing between individuals. It follows, then, that part of the process of developing creativity is the learning and using the facts, skills, and techniques of a subject, or subjects. For the wider the range of experience and knowledge, the more the "equipment" one has to call upon for "immediate apprehension or cognition."

---

[3]Helen Rowan, "The Creative People: How to Spot Them," *Think, op. cit.*, pp. 7-13.

[4]Jerome S. Bruner, *op. cit.*, pp. 57-8. J. P. Guilford, University of Southern California, calls these two types of thinking "divergent thinking" and "convergent thinking."

To go on, Rowan has described the steps of the creative act as (1) preparation, a twofold process of a lifelong amassing of general experience and knowledge and an immediate amassing of specific experience and knowledge concerning the subject to be acted upon; (2) incubation, a step in which there is an active withdrawal from the act (and, some researchers seem to think, in which the subconscious takes over); (3) illumination, a step in which, if it is truly a creative act, intuitive thinking provides a course of action; and, (4) verification, the final testing for the truth of the action, which may involve proving by means of analytical thinking.[5] Of course, the time taken from the conception of the act to the consummation of the act depends on the complexity of the act undertaken. However, the economy of time is a partial measure of the degree of creativeness involved in the action. Again, the time element involved in consummating the act, is also an indication of the "different levels" of experience and knowledge existing between individuals.

There seems to be no doubt in the minds of those investigating creativeness that a broad and deep experience and knowledge is one of the hallmarks of the intuitive thinker. However, there has been an attitude, and it seems to be a holdover from the nineteenth century "genius" concept that such a breadth and depth can be an inhibiting factor in the expression of originality. This attitude seems to be more prevalent in the aesthetic fields than in the practical and scientific. But, one must remember that man is a product of his relationship to the culture of his society, culture being an accumulation of all that has gone before in that society, and that his relevancy is in direct proportion to his relationship to that society. If one isolates himself, to any degree, his position will be a minimal one. Of course, it should be pointed out that any one individual cannot know or experience the totality of a society's culture. But, the greater the acquaintance the more efficient and meaningful will be the action of the individual and, in turn, the greater the contribution of that individual to the present and future of that society. (Note how, again, the "different levels" concept is verified.)

Gordon, reporting for the Synectics Corporation of Cambridge, Massachusetts, sets forth a method for solving problems creatively, which is an example of the exercise of intuition. He outlines the method as being based on four kinds of "Psychological Mechanisms": (1) personal analogy, (2) direct analogy, (3) symbolic analogy, and (4) fantasy

---

[5]Helen Rowan, "How to Produce an Idea," *Think* (International Business Machines Corp.), Vol. 28, No. 10 (Nov.-Dec., 1962), pp. 13-14.

analogy. The first consists of a personal identification with the problem. The second consists of the actual comparison of parallel facts, knowledge or technology. While the third mechanism consists of calling on non-verbal images or symbols to represent the components of the problem. And the last mechanism consists of "turning wish fulfillment into technical invention."[6] Other attempts to increase the creative output, making use of intuitive thinking, are the brainstorming" technique, group dynamics, and "way of life" approach. Whether these techniques have a place in the classroom can be debated, however, it seems these techniques might legitimately be called upon at the teachers' planning table to the ultimate benefit of the student.

Rowan reports that seventy-five percent of the people are sense perceptors. This group concentrates on the facts presented to their five senses in the problem-solving. The other twenty-five percent are intuiters. These persons, in problem-solving, immediately focus their attention on the possibilities.[7] From this it would seem that a fruitful approach in the classroom would be to present and encourage the identification of possibilities, which then can be checked through analytic means. A word of caution: in encouraging the identification of possibilities, the teacher should be alerted to thoughtless "guess and b'gosh," "trial and error" attempts. In this respect, the teacher truly must guide the students to thoughtful possibilities. It goes without saying that these thoughtful possibilities can grow, only out of the student's experience and knowledge. His experience and knowledge are the vehicles of both analytic and intuitive thinking.

Vehicles of Musical Thought

One needs not to be reminded that musical thinking is aural thinking. Properly, musical thinking is the cerebral manipulation of aural images. Past experience and knowledge governs the extensity of an individual's aural imagery.

Seashore has fractionated music into four components: (1) pitch, (2) loudness, (3) time, and (4) timbre.[8] These are the tools, or vehicles, of musical thought and it is with these that aural images are made. Of course, there need be little, or no formal experience or knowledge with these components in order to manipulate the vehicles of

[6]William J. J. Gordon, "How to Get Your Imagination Off the Ground," *Think* (International Business Machines Corp.), Vol. 29, No. 3 (March, 1963), pp. 2-6.
[7]Helen Rowan, *op. cit.*
[8]Carl E. Seashore, *Psychology of Music* (New York: McGraw-Hill Book Co., Inc., 1938), p. 29.

music thought. At best, though, such manipulations are crude and little satisfaction can be derived. Formal experience and knowledge enables the sophisticated and subtle manipulation of these vehicles and, hence, the less crude and the more satisfying to the manipulator.

Resorting to an example: if one's experience and knowledge of pitch is limited to the diatonic scale organization, then one will, in all probability, think, pitch-wise, only within this framework. This may be quite satisfying but the thinker is limited in the ways he can think about pitch and it follows, then, he will be limited in the number of satisfying musical thoughts. Experience and knowledge of many types of pitch organization provides a richer and more varied opportunity for musical thought. So, likewise, with the other three components.

In the Western culture, pitch is organized sequentially, simultaneously, and in sequential-simultaneous combination. Loudness, to a large degree, is organized to create tension or to resolve tension. Time is organized, faster or slower, in duple, triple, or in duple-triple combinations and compounds. Timbre is organized according to the dominance of the individual partials of the over-tone series. Within the framework of the Western culture musical thought, then, consists of the apprehending, comprehending, and manipulating this four-way organization of sound. Creative musical thinking involves such a mastery of this four-way organization that the mode of thought is intuitive as well as analytical.

Training for Creativeness

Can a child be trained to be creative? On first thought, no — but this reflects the extant influence of the nineteenth-century "great man" theory. On second thought, one must answer, yes. That he may not function at the creative level which will command widespread attention may be true, but he can function creatively to satisfy his own needs and desires for beauty. If he can do this, then he will recognize, in a fulfilling way, the higher level creative efforts which will further enhance his satisfaction of the need for beauty.

It has been pointed out that creativeness is a thought process, one that is largely intuitive in manner and to think intuitively is to call upon past experiences, skills, techniques, and knowledge of the materials, tools, and component parts of the subject. So, to train for creativeness in a certain area of endeavor is to identify its materials, tools, and component parts and to build up a backlog of experience, skill, technique, and knowledge of them. In the case of music, they have been defined as the "vehicles of musical thought." Also, these experiences, skills, techniques, and knowledges should be presented in as exciting a manner of problem-solving as is possible in order to develop a curiosity about, and adventuresomeness with the subject. This, then, is the methodology of training for creativeness.

Predicting Success in
Music Teaching

It is generally assumed a music teacher must possess certain basic information, techniques, and skills. Also, music teachers, because of the nature of their subject matter and the unique characteristics of the music curriculum, require certain physical, mental, social, and emotional traits. A survey of the requirements for music teacher certification throughout the United States substantiates this. Obviously, the characteristics necessary for achieving success in one profession are different from those necessary in another profession.

What are the characteristics necessary for achieving success in music teaching? Ryans, in summarizing the answers to this question, lists these characteristics:

> Measured intellectual abilities, achievement in college course, general cultural and special subject-matter knowledge, professional information, student teaching marks, emotional adjustment, attitudes favorable to students, generosity in appraisals of the behavior and motives of other persons, strong interest in reading and literary matters, interest in music and painting, participation in social and community affairs, early experiences in caring for children and teaching (such as reading to children, taking a class for the teacher), history of teaching in family, size of school and size of community in which teaching, cultural level of community and participation in avocational activities, all appear to be characteristics of the teacher which are likely to be positively correlated or associated with teacher effectiveness in the abstract.[1]

---

[1]David G. Ryans, "Prediction of Teacher Effectiveness," *Encyclopedia of Educational Research*, ed. Chester W. Harris (New York: The Macmillan Co., 1960), pp. 1486-91.

The history of investigations concerned with predicting teaching success goes back to Junius Merriam's investigation of *Normal School Education and Efficiency in Teaching* carried out in 1905. From 1905 to around 1930 the problem was investigated by only a few researchers. Odenweller, in reviewing the literature prior to his investigation, listed only ten studies.[2] He concluded that (1) a relationship of about .55 holds between professional knowledge and the quality of teaching and (2) rank in high school class has the most significant relationship to teaching success. He also concluded that (1) intelligence test scores have little validity in predicting successful teaching, and (2) "the least important of forty-five teacher traits is professional preparation."

Barr, in 1948, summarized the research in predicting success[3] and he reviewed the literature appearing between 1948 and 1952.[4] Later, as a capstone to a career centering around the measurement and prediction of teaching success, he reviewed the significant research in this area, dating from Merriam's study of 1905 to 1961.[5] Barr lists six broad attributes which those responsible for the selection of teachers should consider, they are:

1. Intelligence.
2. A thorough knowledge of the subject.
3. Good speech techniques in presenting the subject.
4. Creative imagination.
5. Physical energy and drive.
6. Such personal and moral prerequisites as patience, considerateness, emotional stability, judgment and maturity.[6]

Domas and Tiedeman also published a comprehensive, annotated bibliography of investigation in this area, covering the period from 1905 to 1950.[7]

Determining the attributes necessary to good teaching provides a basis on which to select candidates for teaching and for teacher-training. However, the crux of the problem lies in the determining of the in-

[2]Arthur Leonard Odenweller, "Predicting the Quality of Teaching Success," *Teachers College Contributions to Education*, No. 676 (New York: Bureau of Publications, Teachers College, Columbia University, 1936), pp. 9-14.

[3]A. S. Barr, "The Measurement and Prediction of Teaching Efficiency: A Summary of Investigations," *Journal of Experimental Education*, XVI (June, 1948), pp. 203-83.

[4]————, "The Measurement of Teacher Characteristics and Prediction of Teaching Efficiency," *Review of Educational Research*, XXII (June, 1952), pp. 169-74.

[5]————, ed., "Wisconsin Studies of the Measurement and Prediction of Teacher Effectiveness," *Journal of Experimental Education*, XXX (Sept., 1961), pp. 1-150.

[6]*Ibid.*

[7]Simeon J. Domas and David J. Tiedeman, "Teacher Competence: An Annotated Bibliography," *Journal of Experimental Education*, XIX (Dec., 1950), pp. 101-218.

strument with which these attributes can be measured in relation to success in teaching. Specific measuring instruments for each of the above characteristics have been validated in isolated situations. The most common measuring instruments used are intelligence and scholastic achievement. Personality tests, general culture tests, reading and speech tests, physical and health examinations, interviews, and essays have been tested for their validity in other instances. In an earlier review of the literature on the measurement and prediction of teaching efficiency, Barr suggests:

> Many of the instruments here reported upon have been validated against general criteria of teaching efficiency of various sorts. It would seem desirable to study their relation also to specific functions and aspects of teaching efficiency.[8]

One eminent educator, in making recommendations on the preparation of successful teachers, has written: ". . . . the one indisputably essential element in professional education is practice teaching."[9] Hence, success in practice teaching could be, and has been, used frequently as a criterion of teaching success. Use of such a criterion must be based, at least in part, upon the assumption that "in-service teaching success" is closely related to "practice teaching success." Too few studies have been made of this assumed relationship, obviously because of the difficulties entailed in evaluating in-service teaching performance. Until such studies are forthcoming, the value of this criterion must be accepted largely on faith. The likelihood that exceptional ability in practice teaching is probably followed by above average in-service performance is recognized. Poor practice teaching performance, on the other hand, may very well reflect deficiencies which the student overcomes with experience.

Predicting success in practice teaching has received attention from researchers increasingly since 1929. All types of measures have been tested for their validity. Intelligence, scholastic ability, achievement, aptitude, personality, and general culture tests have all been tested in isolated situations and await further validation. High school grade point average, high school graduating class percentile rank, college grade point averages at several stages of the collegiate career, college major and minor subject grade point averages, and college teacher-training courses' grade point average have also been employed in various situations as predictors of practice teaching success.

---

[8]Barr, "The Measurement and Prediction of Teaching Efficiency . . . ," *op. cit.*
[9]Conant, *op. cit.*, p. 142.

Although the research in predicting practice teaching success is limited, it does have significant implications for further research. Some measures have shown a value in certain instances which should be investigated further, while others have shown little significance to the prediction problem. The review of the research already accomplished also shows a need for investigating those measures of indicated value in relation to specific subject matter areas.

The investigations on predicting teaching success and practice teaching success have been concerned with the discovery of more efficient means to select the personnel to pass on the "interests, purposes, information, skill and practices" of our society. Better selection procedures will, in turn, mean better teachers for the schools of our country.

The need for continued research has been cogently summarized by Stout, Edson and Glatzback, and Charters:

> If we believe that man is educable . . . then we must also believe in the selection of those persons whose intelligence, personality, and attributes best fit them to teach effectively.[10]
>
> Persons in charge of the selection and preparation of teachers have a responsibility to the children who will some day be taught by their students[11]
>
> . . . by carefully selecting students who will teach and who will teach a long time, we can train fewer teachers and, at the same time, get more man-years of teaching from them than currently is the case. Such a selection procedure would make better use of the training facilities in teacher education institutions, permitting higher quality or, at least, more intensive training.[12]

---

[10]Ruth A. Stout, "Admissions and Retention Practices in College Programs of Teacher Education," *Personnel and Guidance Journal,* XXXIV (Dec., 1955), pp. 208-12.

[11]William H. Edson and Charles J. Glatzback, "Recruitment and Selective Admission of the Prospective Teacher," *Guidance in Teacher Education,* 37th Yearbook (The Association for Student Teaching, 1957), pp. 23-40.

[12]W. W. Charters, Jr., "Survival in the Profession: A Criterion for Selecting Teacher Trainees," *Journal of Teacher Education,* VII (Sept., 1956), pp. 253-5.

Part III

RESEARCH
TECHNIQUES

The Development of the Scientific Method

In the search for objective information about, and answers to curricular and instructional problems in music, teachers have appealed, generally, to five sources of information: (1) personal experience, (2) authority, (3) tradition, (4) syllogistic reasoning, and (5) scientific inquiry. These five sources of information represent a brief, chronological outline of the history of man's thought. Music teaching, as a profession, is in the beginning stages of the use of scientific inquiry as a means of determining its curriculum and of solving its instructional problems. Personal experience, authority, and tradition, however, are still the main determinants of the music curriculum and the instructional methods employed. There is, of course, validity in these three sources of information.

Universally, the most used source of information is the personal experience of the teacher. The experienced teacher has learned that certain techniques are successful in his classroom and he employs these techniques again and again. He also will consult local, state, or national authority to solve problems. These sources, too, are often most helpful and reliable. What has been done before is a powerful ally to the music teacher in meeting the challenges in his day-to-day teaching. In fact, few areas of human endeavor cling to their established customs and traditions as tenaciously as does that of the teaching of music. To verify this one needs only to observe any level of music instruction — whether it be elementary, secondary, or collegiate. Valuable as these three sources of information may be, the limiting circumstances attending these sources may produce inefficient, if not inaccurate, solutions.

When man began to investigate the patterns of his own thinking a great advance was made in the efficiency with which he solved his problems. The greatest thought pattern to come from early man was the process of deductive reasoning, developed by Aristotle and perfected by medieval scholars. The chief instrument of deductive reasoning, a process of reasoning from the general to the specific, is syllogism. Syllogism consists of a major premise, a minor premise, and a conclusion, for example: all mankind is essentially good (major premise), AB is a man (minor premise), therefore, AB is good (conclusion). A major weakness in this thought process can be in the premises. This approach to problem solving is not acceptable today, however, it did serve as a "beginning" in establishing a system of objective thinking.

Scientific inquiry, as a method, had its roots in the secularization of the Western World and gained full impetus in the Age of Reason. The method of scientific inquiry is an inductive-deductive mode of thinking — a double movement of thought. First, the researcher collects all the available data and experience concerning a problem. Second, from this collected information he develops a generalization, or hypothesis. This process, from specifics to the general, is the inductive aspect of scientific procedure. Third, the generalization, or hypothesis, is subjected to testing, the tools of which are the data and experiences of known truth. This third process, from the general to the specific, is the deductive aspect of scientific procedure. Thus, the researcher, when proceeding in the scientific manner, starts with known truths to develop a hypothesis and returns to known truths to test the hypothesis in order to develop a new truth. Some characteristics of scientific procedure are: it is based on known truths, it makes use of analysis, it employs quantitative methods in interpreting data and experience, and it is free from bias. In summary, the steps in scientific inquiry are the preliminary observation of facts, the formulation of a hypothesis from this observation, and the testing of the hypothesis. John Dewey has elaborated on these three steps:

Steps in Reflective Thinking
1. The occurrence of a felt difficulty:
   a. in the lack of adapting to a means to an end;
   b. in identifying the character of an object;
   c. in explaining an unexpected event.
2. Definition of the difficulty in terms of problem statement.
3. Occurrence of a suggested explanation or possible solution — a guess, inference, theory, i.e., a hypothesis.

4. A rational elaboration of the suggested explanation by means of collecting data (evidence).
5. Corroboration of the idea and formation of a concluding belief through experimental verification of the hypothesis.[1]

---

[1]John Dewey, *How We Think* (Boston: D. C. Heath and Co., 1933), p. 12.

The Nature of Research

There are, without a doubt, more unsolved than solved problems in the teaching of music. With such variable factors as the student's physical being, mental capacity, emotional well-being, and social concern; the school's academic and administrative organization; and the community's economic, social, and moral conditions there will always be questions to ask and answers to be sought. Human behavior, and that is what education is — the interaction of the behavior of human beings, is a highly complex pattern of action and cannot be dealt with in the very simple quantitative terms. That is not to say, however, that quantitative terms cannot be employed in the search for answers to educational problems, but, they must be used in a highly sophisticated manner.

What is a research problem? (Such a simple question!) It is the "felt difficulty" — to borrow from John Dewey's "Steps in Reflective Thinking" — identified. (Such a simple answer!) Many of the identifiable "felt difficulties" are solved by referring to personal experience, authority, or tradition. Others require more concerted, sophisticated action, that is, scientific procedure. Many "felt difficulties" stem from one's own day-to-day activity and need be solved in order to proceed with the day-to-day activity. The solving of such problems falls in the realm of applied research.[1] Other "felt difficulties" do not relate to day-to-day activity and need to be solved only because they are a

---

[1]There is an interesting discussion of this type of research which is called, by the author, "action research" in: Pernecky, Jack M. "Action Research Methodology." *Bulletin* No. 1 (1963), Council for Research in Music Education. pp. 33-37.

source of challenge, in other words, "the mountain must be climbed because it is there." The solving of these kinds of problems can be categorized as pure research.

Identifying a Problem

Those noted for their successful research are not ones who shrug their shoulders and hope the problem will disappear, but are highly sensitive, curious, adventuresome persons, willing to accept the challenge of solving the problem. They are the ones who are sensitive to the difficulties arising out of day-to-day activity — who are challenged to do something about these difficulties. They are the ones who, early in their careers, have become curious about a particular area of endeavor and are satisfying that curiosity through an organized program of reading the literature, both published and unpublished, pertaining to that area of endeavor. They are the ones who, respecting tradition for what it offers, are adventuresome enough to try the untried. This description of a successful researcher, then, could also serve as a guide to the inexperienced in "finding" — "locating" a research problem. Good and Scates are more specific in their directions on locating a research problem, they are:

1. Published studies
2. Authoritative statements
3. Discussions of current trends
4. Prophecies of future developments
5. Lists of studies and theses in progress
6. Outlines of problems for investigation[2]

The above-mentioned authors, directing their discussion to prospective master's thesis and doctoral dissertation writers, list several factors which a propective researcher should consider in his selection of a problem. Again, being very specific, they are:

1. Novelty and avoidance of unnecessary duplication
2. Importance for the field represented and implementation
3. Interest, intellectual curiosity and drive
4. Training and personal qualifications
5. Availability of data and method
6. Special equipment and working conditions
7. Sponsorship and administrative cooperation

---

[2]Carter V. Good and Douglas E. Scates, *Methods of Research* (New York: Appleton-Century-Crofts, Inc., 1954), p. 43.

8. Costs and returns
9. Hazards, penalties, and handicaps
10. Time factor[3]

The present writers maintain that, if their three-fold criteria, that is, sensitivity, curiosity, and adventuresomeness, are present in the potential researcher, there will be more than a sufficient number of "felt difficulties" identified. True, many of these identified "felt difficulties" are minor and will be solved from personal experience, authority, or tradition. But the fewer ones, the major ones, which defy less sophisticated problem-solving techniques will be so challenging to the sensitive, curious, adventuresome person that he will overcome many of the practical considerations such as lack of experience and training, time, money, and equipment in order to meet the challenge successfully.

Delimiting a Problem

To insure future, orderly procedure in attacking a problem one must state the problem as succinctly and precisely as possible. It should be an all-encompassing statement, but not so much so that it is a general statement and is not completely applicable to the situation or environment which produced the problem in the first place. It should also be specific enough to be a guide for the collecting of data for use in its solution. Obviously, the statement must be one which can be subjected to rigorous testing.

Survey of Related Materials

Having accepted the challenge of a problem, the would-be problem-solver should embark on a well-planned, well-organized program of reading which encompasses *all* the literature directly, and indirectly, concerning the problem. Most obviously, such a reading program will inform the researcher whether the problem has been solved; if so, what methods and techniques were employed in the solution; if not, what attempts, if any, have been made to solve the problem; what, if any, parallel problems have been solved or attempted to be solved; what data is already available for the solution of the problem. Such a reading program, known to the experienced researcher as a "survey of related material," requires considerable bibliographic techniques. (The following section attempts to delineate some of these techniques.) A report of

---

[3]*Ibid.*, p. 49.

the "survey of related material" usually constitutes one of the first sections of the final research report of the problem solved.

Solving the Problem

Music, as one aspect of the culture of a society, is, thus, one aspect of human behavior. So, the study of its effect upon human beings, or the manner in which human beings create music, is in the realm of the behavioral sciences. The history of research in music behavior, as well as that of the other behavioral sciences, does not span many years, in fact, the span covers only the late nineteenth and twentieth centuries. Two significant works, and among the first, on musical behavior are Carl Seashore's *The Psychology of Musical Talent,* published in 1919, and Max Weber's *The Rational and Social Foundations of Music,* published in Munich in 1921.[4] These two pioneers have inspired much of the research in musical behavior which since has been accomplished.

If the research on musical behavior is to be considered scientific it must be carried on and reported in a scientific manner. The characteristics of such research embody a detailed description of what was done and how it was done; definitions which are exacting and precise; an objective collection of data; and, results which are replicable. If such research is to be meaningful to the music profession it must be accomplished by members of the profession.[5] These members must acquire the outlook of the true scientist. The true scientist is not concerned with value judgments of right or wrong, good or bad, but with what is true or false. The true scientist accepts the possibility of anything, but he does not accept it as truth until it is so proven.

The design of research in musical behavior is related to both the behavioral sciences and educational methodology. Education textbooks usually include these designs in their discussions of the design of research: historical, descriptive, philosophical, prognostic, sociological, case-study, curricular, and experimental. There is, however, considerable "overlapping" in the preceding list. The behavioral sciences have used the descriptive-survey, the experimental, and the case-study designs as

---

[4]This work has been reprinted by the Southern Illinois University Press, Carbondale, Ill., 1958.

[5]Charles Leonhard, in discussing one aspect of musical behavior, says, "Music education must develop from within its own ranks people who are competent to carry on rigorous experimental research on musical learning. Up to the present time, most of the research in musical learning has been the work of psychologists who happened to be interested in music." ("Newer Concepts in Learning Theory as They Apply to Music Education," *Bulletin* No. 1, 1963, Council for Research in Music Education, p. 30.)

the basic designs of problem-solving. That is not to say, it should be noted, that the behavioral sciences have not utilized the historical design, for they have. This design has its particular value to the behaviorist in the comparison of data and in demonstrating cause-effect. The present writers choose to divide research design into four broad categories, they are: descriptive-survey, experimental, case-study, and historical.[6]

Descriptive-Survey Design

A descriptive-survey design is that design which subjects evidence (facts, data, events, conditions, etc.) to any or all of the procedures of scrutiny (describing, inspecting, recounting, characterizing, classifying, etc.) for the purpose of providing precise, accurate, exacting information. Besides the usual bibliographical tools such as dictionaries, encyclopedias, reports, and documents, such tools as questionnaires, interviews, and observations are useful to the researcher in the accumulation of his evidence. Just what the specific procedure of scrutiny may be is left to the researcher's choice,[7] however, to what extent the information he gleans is truthful depends on the fine degree of scrutiny to which he subjects his evidence.

Experimental Design

An experimental design is that design which employs an act, operation, trial, or test to determine the truthfulness of a statement or principle. In the act, operation, trial, or test an attempt is made to maintain control of all important elements except one which is manipulated, managed, or handled in order to determine and measure the effect of the manipulating, managing, or handling so that the truthfulness of the statement may be determined. Again, the sophistication with which the researcher manipulates, manages, or handles the one element will affect the extent of the truthfulness. Also, the extent to which the elements represent universality affects the universality of the determined truthfulness. A popular example of this design is represented by the choosing of two identical groups; then, subjecting one group to a particular manipulating, managing, or handling; and, then, comparing the groups. If there is now a difference as a result of the

---

[6]These categories coincide with Good and Scates (*op. cit.*) divisions. Also, the writers intend no order of importance in their listing.

[7]With the common availability of computers, a most popular tool in the procedure of scrutiny, at the present time, is the statistical.

manipulating, managing, or handling, then the statement or principle represented by that action possesses truth — the degree of truth depends on the sophistication of the action and the universality represented by the two groups.

Case-Study Design

A case-study design is that design which involves the consideration of pertinent facts — most usually gained from observation, interviews, and testing — about an individual, or group, in order to identify the determinants of the status and the status, itself, of the individual, or group. Here, too, the degree of sophistication involved in the consideration determines the extent of truthfulness of the status and of the determinants of the status. And here, again, the degree to which the individual, or group, represents the larger population determines the degree of truthfulness about the larger population which may be inferred from the individual, or group.

Historical Design

The historical design is that design which is a report of past events, together with a critical evaluation, from the vantage point of time-distance, of those events in order to find the truth, or a truth, about those events. A narrative of events, as monumental and difficult a task as that may be to accomplish, which does not include a critical evaluation, is not, strictly speaking, within the framework of historical design. It is in this area of critical evaluation that the researcher encounters difficulty. The novice in history too often does not realize there are different viewpoints which may be adopted in the critical evaluation of past events. That is not to say he does not have a viewpoint, but it is a viewpoint stemming from his own accumulation of past experiences of which he is largely unaware. Good and Scates,[8] summarizing the viewpoints discussed by Allen Nevins,[9] lists seven principle viewpoints which have been taken in the critical evaluation of past events, they are:

1. The "great man"
2. The spiritual or idealistic
3. The scientific or technological
4. The economic

---

[8]*Op. cit.*, pp. 215-6.
[9]Allen Nevins, *The Gateway to History* (Boston: D. C. Heath and Co., 1938). Also, the following should be consulted for theories and philosophies of history as applied to music: Allen, William Dwight. *Philosophies of Music History*. New York: Dover Publications, Inc., 1962.

5. The geographic
6. The sociological
7. The eclectic, or "cultural epochs"

It is in the sensitive area of critical evaluation that the whole basis of the truth which is being sought rests — on which the truth will be accepted or rejected. Also, it should be repeated again and again, the basis for sound historical research rests in a sound command of bibliographic techniques.

Bibliographic Techniques

In the previous section it has been stressed "a sound command of bibliographic techniques" is essential for the carrying-on of research. Knowing how and where to locate the information one needs is a necessary skill. It well-behooves the music research student to cultivate such skills.

Locating Information

Obviously, the greatest storehouse of information is the library. Knowing the cataloging system of the library is the first requisite to the efficient collecting of information. Here, in the United States, one or the other of two systems is employed[1] — the Dewey Decimal System, the older, and the Library of Congress System. Following, is a summary of the two systems:[2]

Dewey Decimal System		*Library of Congress System*	
000	General works	A	General works — polygraphy
100	Philosophy	B	Philosophy — religion
200	Religion	C	History — auxiliary sciences
300	Sociology	D	Universal and old world
400	Philology		history
500	Pure Science	E, F	America
600	Useful arts.	G	Geography — Anthropology
	Applied Science	H	Social sciences —

---

[1] A third system, the Cutter System, was employed in a limited number of libraries.

[2] Margaret Mann, *Introduction to Cataloging and the Classification of Books* (Chicago: American Library Association, 1930), pp. 66 and 95-6.

700	Fine Arts		Economics —
800	Literature.		Sociology
	Belles-lettres	J	Political science
900	History.	K	Law
	Biography	L	Education
		M	Music
		N	Fine Arts
		P	Language and Literature
		Q	Science
		R	Medicine
		S	Agriculture — plant and animal industry
		T	Technology
		U	Military science
		V	Naval science
		Z	Bibliography and Library science

The second requisite to the efficient collecting of information is in knowing which sources of information will supply him the necessary facts in the quickest, most authoritative manner. Two of the most useful tools to the music researcher, in determining which sources will be most useful to him, are:

> Winchell, Constance M. *Guide to Reference Books,* 8th ed. Chicago: American Library Association, 1967.
> This is the standard tool for all those concerned with, and about, reference books.

> Duckles, Vincent. *Music Reference and Research Materials: An Annotated Bibliography.* Glencoe: The Free Press of Glencoe, 1964.
> This is the standard tool for all those concerned with, and about, reference materials in music; especially so to the music historian.

Besides the two above-mentioned most valuable tools, the following classified bibliography will be of great service to the researcher involved in "music education" research.

Subject Headings Listing

Sears, Minnie E. *Sears List of Subject Headings,* 6th ed., rev. Bertha M. Frick. New York: H. W. Wilson Co., 1950.

Book Listings for the United States

before 1875
Preface, *The United States Catalog*
1876-1910
American Catalogue of Books, 1876-1910. New York: Office of the Publishers' Weekly, 1876-1910.
1898-1928
The United States Catalog, 4th ed. New York: H. W. Wilson Co., 1928.
1928 to present
The Cumulative Book Index, supplements to *The United States Catalog.*
Previous few weeks
Publishers' Weekly. New York: R. R. Bowker Co.

Locating Books Not in Researcher's Library

ed. Downs, Robert B. *Union Catalogs in the United States.* Chicago: American History Association, 1942.
Downs, Robert B. *American Library Resources: A Bibliography Guide.* Chicago: American Library Association, 1951.

Abstracts and Periodical Indexes, Selected List

Annual Library Index, 1905-1910, ed. William I. Fletcher & H. E. Haines, *et al.* New York: Office of the Publishers' Weekly, 1906-1911.
Annual Literary Index, 1892-1904, ed. William I. Fletcher & R. R. Bowker, *et al.* New York: Office of the Publishers' Weekly, 1893-1905.
Annual Magazine Subject-Index. Boston: The F. W. Faxon Co., 1907-.
Art Index. New York: H. W. Wilson Co., 1930-.
Bibliographic Index. New York: H. W. Wilson Co., 1938-.
Biography Index. New York: H. W. Wilson Co., 1946-.
Book Review Digest. New York: H. W. Wilson Co., 1905-.
Catholic Periodical Index. Washington, D. C.: Catholic Library Association, 1930-.

Child Development Abstracts and Bibliography. Evanston: Northwestern University, 1927-.

Dramatic Index. Boston: The F. W. Faxon Co., 1910-.

Education Abstracts. Bloomington, Ind.: Phi Delta Kappa, 1937-1944.

Education Index. New York: H. W. Wilson Co., 1929-.

Facts on File: Weekly World News Digest with Cumulative Index. New York: Facts on File, 1940-.

Guidance Index. Chicago: Science Research Associates, 1938-.

Library Literature. New York: H. W. Wilson Co., 1933-.

Music Index. Detroit: Information Service, Inc., 1949-.

Occupational Index. Peapack, N. J.: Personnel Services. 1936-.

Poole's Index to Periodical Literature, 1802-1881, 3rd ed., rev. Boston: Houghton Mifflin Co., 1891.

Psychological Abstracts. Lancaster, Pa.: American Psychological Association, 1927-.

Psychological Index. Princeton: Psychological Review Co., 1894-1935.

Public Affairs Information Service Bulletin. New York: Public Affairs Information Service, 1915-.

Readers' Guide to Periodical Literature. New York: H. W. Wilson Co., 1900-.

Record of Current Educational Publications. Washington, D. C.: United States Government Printing Office, 1912-1932.

Social Science Abstracts. New York: Social Science Abstracts, Inc., 1929-1933.

Sociological Abstracts. New York: Sociological Abstracts, 1953-.

State Law Index. Washington, D. C.: Library of Congress, 1929-1952.

Vertical File Index. New York: H. W. Wilson Co., 1932-.

Lists and Data on Individual Periodicals

America's Educational Press. Washington, D. C.: Educational Press Association of America, 1926-.

Monroe, W. S., Thomas T. Hamilton, & V. T. Smith. *Selected List of Educational Periodicals*, Bulletin No. 50, University of Illinois. Urbana: University of Illinois Press, 1930.

Directory of Newspapers and Periodicals. Philadelphia: N. W. Ayer & Son, Inc., 1880-.

Ulrich, Carolyn F. *Periodicals Directory*. New York: R. R. Bowker Co., 1932-.

Locating Periodicals Not in Researcher's Library

Union List of Serials in Libraries of the United States and Canada. New York: H. W. Wilson Co., 1943-1953.

Union List of Technical Periodicals, 3rd ed., comp. Elizabeth G. Bowerman. New York: Special Libraries Association, 1947.

Almanacs

Information Please Almanac. New York: The Macmillan Co., 1947-.
World Almanac. New York: New York World-Telegram, 1868-.

Special Days and Events

Douglas, George W. *The American Book of Days,* 2nd ed., rev. Helen Douglas Compton. New York: H. W. Wilson Co., 1948.

Kane, Joseph N. *Famous First Facts.* New York: H. W. Wilson Co., 1955.

Carruth, Gorton & Associates. *Encyclopedia of American Facts and Dates.* New York: Thomas Y. Crowell Co., 1956.

Bibliographies on Education

Monroe, Walter S. & Louis Shores. *Bibliographies and Summaries in Education to July 1, 1935.* New York: H. W. Wilson Co., 1936.

Dictionaries on Education

ed. Good, Carter V. *Dictionary of Education.* New York: McGraw-Hill Book Co., Inc., 1945.

Encyclopedias on Education

ed. Monroe, Paul. *Cyclopedia of Education.* New York: The Macmillan Co., 1911-1913.

ed. Rivlin, Harry N. & Herbert Schueler. *Encyclopedia of Modern Education.* New York: Philosophical Library, 1943.

ed. Monroe, Walter S. *Encyclopedia on Educational Research,* rev. ed. New York: The Macmillan Co., 1950.

Statistics on Education

Biennial Survey of Education in the United States 1916/1918-. Washington, D. C.: United States Government Printing Office, 1919-.

Yearbooks on Education

Yearbook of the National Society for the Study of Education. Chicago: University of Chicago Press, 1902-.

The Year Book of Education. Cleveland: World Book Co., 1932-1940, 1948-.

ed. Kandel, I. L. *Educational Yearbook.* New York: Bureau of Publications, Teachers College, Columbia University, 1922-1944.

Government Manuals

Federal

United States Government Organization Manual. Washington, D. C.: United States Government Printing Office, 1935-.

State

The Book of the States. Chicago: The Council of State Governments, 1935-.

Local

The Municipal Year Book. Chicago: International City Managers' Association, 1934-.

International

The Statesman's Year-Book. New York: The Macmillan Co., 1864-.

Statistics, noneducational

Statistical Abstract of the United States. Washington, D. C.: United States Government Printing Office, 1878-.

Handbook of Basic Economic Statistics. Washington, D. C.: United States Government Printing Office, 1947-.

Economic Almanac. New York: Thomas Y. Crowell Co., 1940-.

Yearbooks, noneducational

American Yearbook. New York: Thomas Nelson & Sons, 1910-1919, 1925-.

Office of Education, Department of Health, Education, and Welfare, Publications (all printed by the United States Government Printing Office, Washington, D. C.)

Before 1910

List of Publications of the United States Bureau of Education, 1867-1910. Bulletin No. 3, 1910.

1910-1936

List of Publications of the United States Office of Education, 1910-1936: Including Those of the Former Federal Board for Vocational Education for 1917-1933. Bulletin No. 22, 1937.

After 1936
> *Bulletins of the Bureau of Education, 1906-1927.* Bulletin No. 17, 1928.
>
> *Educational Directory.* 1912-.
>
> *United States Office of Education and Other Publications Relating to Education. Price List.*
>
> *School Life.* 1918-.

Government Documents

> Hirshberg, Herbert S. & Carl H. Melinat. *Subject Guide to United States Government Publications.* Chicago: American Library Association, 1947.

Federal, before 1881 (all printed by the United States Government Printing Office, Washington, D. C., unless otherwise noted)

> Poore, B. P. *A Descriptive Catalogue of the Government Publications of the United States, 1774-1881.*

Federal, between 1881-1893

> Ames, J. G. *Comprehensive Index to the Publications of the United States Government, 1881-1893.*

Federal, between 1893-1940

> *Document Catalog.* 1893-1940.
>
> *Document Index.* 1897-1933.

Federal, between 1941-1950

> *United States Government Publications, Monthly Catalog: Decennial Cumulative Index, 1941-1950.* 1953.

Federal, 1950 to present

> *United States Government Publications, Monthly Catalog.* 1895-.
>
> *Selected United States Government Publications.* 1928-.
>
> Jackson, Ellen. *A Manual for the Administration of the Federal Documents.* Chicago: American Library Association, 1955.
>
> Temple, Phillips. *Federal Services to Libraries.* Chicago: American Library Association, 1954.

State

> Wilcox, Jerome K. *Manual on the Use of State Publications.* Chicago: American Library Association, 1940.

State, before 1910

> Bowker, R. R. *State Publications: A Provisional List of the Official Publications of the Several States of the United States from their Organization.* New York: Publishers' Weekly, 1899-1909.

State, since 1910
> Monthly Checklist of State Publications. Washington, D. C.:
> United States Government Printing Office, 1910-.

Local
> Hodgson, James Goodwin. The Official Publications of American
> Counties, A Union List. Fort Collins, Colo.: J. G. Hodgson,
> 1937.
> Checklist of Basic Municipal Documents. Washington, D. C.:
> United States Government Printing Office, 1948.

Biography

Current Biography. New York: H. W. Wilson Co., 1940-.

ed. Cattel, Jacques. Directory of American Scholars. Lancaster, Pa.:
The Science Press, 1942-.

Who's Who in America. Chicago: A. N. Marquis Co., 1899-.

Who Was Who in America. Chicago: A. N. Marquis Co., 1943-.

ed. Cattel, Jacques. American Men of Science. New York: R. R.
Bowker Co., 1927-.

ed. Cook, Robert C. & Mary Alice Smith. Who's Who in American
Education. Nashville: Who's Who in American Education, 1928-.

Research in Education

1918-1927
> Monroe, Walter S. Ten Years of Educational Research, 1918-1927.
> Bulletin No. 42, Bureau of Educational Research, University of
> Illinois. Urbana: University of Illinois Press, 1928.

1926-1940
> Bibliography of Research Studies in Education, Office of Edu-
> cation. Washington, D. C.: United States Government Print-
> ing Office, 1926-1941.

1941-1952
> Lyda, Mary Louise & Stanley B. Brown. Research Studies in Edu-
> cation, A Subject Index of Doctoral Dissertations, Reports,
> and Field Studies, 1941-1951. Boulder, Colo.: Beta Delta Chap-
> ter, Phi Delta Kappa, 1953.
> Lyda, Mary Louise & Stanley B. Brown. Research Studies in Edu-
> cation, A Subject Index, 1952. Boulder, Colo.: Beta Delta
> Chapter, Phi Delta Kappa, 1954.

1953 to present
> Lyda, Mary Louise, Stanley B. Brown, & Carter V. Good. Research
> Studies in Education, A Subject Index. Bloomington, Ind.:
> Phi Delta Kappa, Inc.

Theses and Dissertations
> *A list of American Doctoral Dissertations.* Washington, D. C.:
> United States Government Printing Office, 1912-1938.
> *Doctoral Dissertations Accepted by American Universities.*
> New York: H. W. Wilson Co., 1934-1955.
> *Dissertation Abstracts and Index to American Doctoral Disser-*
> *tations.* Ann Arbor: University Microfilms, 1938-.

Documenting Information

On locating pertinent information, detailed bibliographic data and a brief summary and evaluation of the information must be taken. For this purpose a flexible, but permanent system should be devised. Note cards (3″ x 5″, 4″ x 6″, or larger file cards) are very efficient in that they may be easily shuffled in order to classify the contents in any manner necessary. Just as efficient is punched paper, in any size, which can be kept in a loose-leaf notebook, which can also be shuffled to meet the momentary classification demands. Any system of recording bibliographic data, summaries, and evaluations which does not permit the insertion of new materials into that classification system, or the fast re-classification, is too restrictive to the efficient handling of such information.

In summarizing information, all pertinent arguments should be recorded and a brief evaluation of these arguments made. It is time-consuming going back to the original source to clarify a summarization. (Needless to say, all recording of information onto note cards or note papers should be done in a completely legible manner.) If it does become necessary to refer to the original source, it is even more frustrating not to have taken complete bibliographical data. Such data consists of author's complete identification, title of source (edition, editor, or translator), place of publication, publisher, copyright year, and volume and page numbers. (The authors have found it expeditious to record somewhere on the note card, in a uniform position, the library where the book was found and its call number, for example:

IaU
ML552. The IaU tells them the book was used in the University of Iowa
W72
Library and the University of Iowa Library's call number for that book

is $\frac{\text{ML552}}{\text{W72}}$.

Bibliographic data should always be recorded in a consistent manner and, since these data will eventually be listed in a formal bibliography, the style of recording should be the same as that used in the formal bibliography. (It is quite expedient to arrange the note cards, finally, in alphabetical order, according to the first entry of the bibliographical data, and then work from the cards in developing the formal bibliography.) There are several styles of recording and the prospective researcher is urged to adopt one style and use it consistently. Following is a style which has proved efficient for the authors: author's last name — comma — author's first and second names, or initials — period — title of book (comma — edition, editor, or translator) — period — place of publication — colon — publisher — comma — copyright date — period — page number, or numbers — period. Below, consistent with this style, are some examples of the way to record bibliographical data which present slightly different recording problems (since the problem of footnoting is so closely related the examples are also written in footnote style for the purposes of comparison — the first example is in bibliography style, the second in footnote style).

Complete Book Cited

Single author

>Kaplan, Max. *Foundations and Frontiers of Music Education.* New York: Holt, Rinehart and Winston, Inc., 1966.

>Max Kaplan, *Foundations and Frontiers of Music Education* (New York: Holt, Rinehart and Winston, Inc., 1966), p. 10.

>Shetler, Donald J. *Film Guide for Music Educators.* Washington, D. C.: Music Educators National Conference, 1961.

>Donald J. Shetler, *Film Guide for Music Educators* (Washington, D. C.: Music Educators National Conference, 1961), p. 11.

Same author (in bibliography style, list succeeding titles by the same author, omitting author's name and, instead, underline seven spaces followed by a period; in footnote style, use *ibid.*, plus page number.)

>————. *Film Guide for Music Educators.* Washington, D. C.: Music Educators National Conference, 1961.

>*Ibid.,* p. 12.

Pseudonym of author noted

>Heseltine, Philip (pseudonym Peter Warlock). *Frederick Delius.* London: The Bodley Head, Ltd., 1923.

Philip Heseltine (pseudonym Peter Warlock), *Frederick Delius* (London: The Bodley Head, Ltd., 1923), p. 13.

Author anonymous

Anonymous. *Christian Psalmody.* Boston: Samuel T. Armstrong, 1825.

Anonymous, *Christian Psalmody* (Boston: Samuel T. Armstrong, 1825), p. 14.

Choral Latin. London: National Federation of Music Societies, n.d.
Choral Latin (London: National Federation of Music Societies, n.d.), p. 15.

Edition noted

Piston, Walter. *Harmony,* 3rd ed. New York: W. W. Norton & Co., Inc., 1962.

Walter Piston, *Harmony,* 3rd ed. (New York: W. W. Norton & Co., Inc., 1962), p. 16.

Editor and author

Ives, Charles. *Essays Before a Sonata and Other Writings,* Howard Boatwright, editor. New York: W. W. Norton & Co., Inc., 1961.

Charles Ives, *Essays Before a Sonata and Other Writings,* Howard Boatwright, editor. (New York: W. W. Norton & Co., Inc., 1961), p. 17.

Editor as author

Kraus, Egon, editor. *Comparative Music Education.* Mainz: B. Schotts' Sohne, 1962.

Egon Kraus, editor, *Comparative Music Education* (Mainz: B. Schotts' Sohne, 1962), p. 18.

Knapp, J. Merrill, editor. *Selected List of Music for Men's Voices.* Princeton: Princeton University Press, 1952.

J. Merrill Knapp, editor, *Selected List of Music for Men's Voices* (Princeton: Princeton University Press, 1952), p. 19.

Organization as author

National Interscholastic Music Activities Commission. *NIMAC Manual.* Washington, D. C.: Music Educators National Conference, 1963.

National Interscholastic Music Activities Commission, *NIMAC Manual* (Washington, D. C.: Music Educators National Conference, 1963), p. 20.

Joint authorship

>Leonhard, Charles and Robert W. House. *Foundations and Principles of Music Education.* New York: McGraw-Hill Book Co., Inc., 1959.

>Charles Leonhard and Robert W. House, *Foundations and Principles of Music Education* (New York: McGraw-Hill Book Co., Inc., 1959), p. 21.

Series noted

>Nordholm, Harriet. *Singing in the Elementary Schools* (Foundations of Music Education Series, Allen P. Britton, editor). Englewood Cliffs: Prentice-Hall, Inc., 1966.

>Harriet Nordholm, *Singing in the Elementary Schools,* Foundations of Music Education Series, Allen P. Britton, editor. (Englewood Cliffs: Prentice-Hall, Inc., 1966), p. 22.

Translator(s) noted

>Rinderer, Leo and Egon Kraus, Rudolph Schock, and Hilmar Höckner. *Music Education: A Handbook for Music Teaching in the Elementary Grades,* translated by Edmund A. Cykler and John R. Keith. Park Ridge: Neil A. Kjos Music Co., 1961.

>Leo Rinderer, Egon Kraus, Rudolph Schock, and Hilmar Höckner, *Music Education: A Handbook for Music Teaching in the Elementary Grades,* translated by Edmund A. Cykler and John R. Keith (Park Ridge: Neil A. Kjos Music Co., 1961), p. 23.

Volumes noted

>Hughes, Dom Anselm and Gerald Abraham, editors. *Ars Nova and the Renaissance,* Vol. III of *The New Oxford History of Music.* London: Oxford University Press, 1960.

>Dom Anselm Hughes and Gerald Abraham, editors, *Ars Nova and the Renaissance,* Vol. III of *The New Oxford History of Music* (London: Oxford University Press, 1960), p. 24.

>Finn, William J. *The Art of the Choral Conductor,* 2 vols. Evanston: Summy-Birchard Publishing Co., 1960.

>William J. Finn, *The Art of the Choral Conductor* (Evanston: Summy-Birchard Publishing Co., 1960), vol. I, p. 25.

Part of Book Cited with Title of Part

>Hood, Mantle. "Music, the Unknown." *Musicology* (The Princeton Studies, Richard Schlatter, editor). Englewood Cliffs: Prentice-Hall, Inc., 1963.

Mantle Hood, "Music, the Unknown," *Musicology,* The Princeton
Studies, Richard Schlatter, editor. (Englewood Cliffs: Pren-
tice-Hall, Inc., 1963), p. 26.

Yearbook or Bulletin
Whole noted and author cited
Palisca, Claude V. *Music in Our Schools: A Search for Improve-
ment.* U. S. Department of Health, Education, and Welfare,
Office of Education Bulletin 1964, No. 28.
Claude V. Palisca, *Music in Our Schools: A Search for Improve-
ment* (U. S. Department of Health, Education, and Welfare,
Office of Education Bulletin 1964, No. 28), p. 27.

Morgan, Hazel Nohavec, editor. *Music in American Education,*
Music Education Source Book No. 2. Washington, D. C.:
Music Educators National Conference, 1955.
Hazel Nohavec Morgan, editor, *Music In American Education,*
Music Education Source Book No. 2 (Washington, D. C.:
Music Educators National Conference, 1955), p. 28.

Whole noted and no author cited
The Music Curriculum in Secondary Schools. Bulletin (March,
1959) of the National Association of Secondary-School Prin-
cipals. Reprinted by the Music Educators National Conference,
1959.
The Music Curriculum in Secondary Schools (Bulletin, March,
1959, of the National Association of Secondary-School Prin-
cipals, reprinted by the Music Educators National Conference,
1959), p. 29.

Part noted and author of part cited
Thorpe, Louis P. "Learning Theory and Music Teaching." *Basic
Concepts in Music Education.* The Fifty-seventh Yearbook of
the National Society for the Study of Education, Part I. Chicago: University of Chicago Press, 1958.
Louis P. Thorpe, "Learning Theory and Music Teaching," *Basic
Concepts in Music Education* (The Fifty-seventh Yearbook of
the National Society for the Study of Education, Part I. Chicago: University of Chicago Press, 1958), p. 165.

Encyclopedia and Dictionary

Author and article noted

> Shaw, Harold Watkins. "Tonic Sol-fa." *Grove's Dictionary of Music and Musicians,* 5th ed., Eric Blom, editor. New York: St. Martin's Press, 1954.
>
> Harold Watkins Shaw, "Tonic Sol-fa," *Grove's Dictionary of Music and Musicians,* 5th ed., Eric Blom, editor. (New York: St. Martin's Press, 1954), vol. VIII, p. 504.

Article, but no author, noted

> "Education and Music." *The Oxford Companion to Music,* 9th ed. New York: Oxford University Press, 1955.
>
> "Education and Music," *The Oxford Companion to Music,* 9th ed. (New York: Oxford University Press, 1955), p. 315.

No author or article noted

> *Baker's Biographical Dictionary of Musicians,* 5th ed. rev., Nicolas Slonimsky, editor. New York: G. Schirmer, Inc., 1965.
>
> *Baker's Biographical Dictionary of Musicians,* 5th ed. rev., Nicolas Slonimsky, editor. (New York: G. Schirmer, Inc., 1965), p. 33.

Newspaper Article

Author noted

> Strongin, Theodore. "35,000 Turn Back Clock at Park Concert." *The New York Times,* June 23, 1966.
>
> Theodore Strongin, "35,000 Turn Back Clock at Park Concert" (*The New York Times,* June 23, 1966), p. 34.

Author not noted

> "S O S From Moscow Brings Music By Air." *The New York Times,* June 25, 1966.
>
> "S O S From Moscow Brings Music By Air" (*The New York Times,* June 25, 1966), p. 35.

Periodical Article

Author noted

> Fuller, Buckminster. "The Music of the New Life." *Music Educators Journal,* 52/6 (June-July, 1966).
>
> Buckminster Fuller, "The Music of the New Life" (*Music Educators Journal,* June-July, 1966), p. 36.
>
> Longyear, R. M. "Schiller and Opera." *The Musical Quarterly,* LII/2 (April, 1966).

R. M. Longyear, "Schiller and Opera" (*The Musical Quarterly,* April, 1966), p. 37.

Author not noted

"Composers: Goodbye to All That." *Time,* 87/25 (June 24, 1966).
"Composers: Goodbye to All That" (*Time,* June 24, 1966), p. 62.

Theses and Dissertations

Gray, Thomas Leighton. *An Investigation in Teaching Concepts of Student Teachers of Music.* Unpublished doctoral dissertation, University of Iowa, 1962.

Thomas Leighton Gray, *An Investigation in Teaching Concepts of Student Teachers of Music* (unpublished doctoral dissertation, University of Iowa, 1962), p. 38.

Reporting

A researcher has the responsibility of sharing the results of his research with his colleagues. This involves the writing of a final report. Such a report usually is divided into five sections: (1) statement of the problem, its limitations, and the need for the solution; (2) survey of materials related to the problem; (3) a description of the procedures of solution; (4) results of the problem solving; and (5) conclusions and recommendations for future action.

A final research report should be "long enough to cover the subject but, brief enough to be interesting." The style of writing should be simple, concise, and to-the-point — it goes without saying that the rules of grammar, punctuation, and spelling should be observed, scrupulously (one who is careless in these details will convey the impression he was careless in his research). The format of the report will vary according to the demands of the institution, periodical, or book publisher to whom the reporter may submit his report. Each of these agencies will have "style manuals" which they will supply upon request. The authors also recommend the following as being especially helpful in writing final research reports:

Strunk, Jr., William and E. B. White. *The Elements of Style.* New York: The Macmillan Co., 1959.

Turabian, Kate L. *A Manual for Writers of Term Papers, Theses, and Dissertations.* Chicago: University of Chicago Press, 1955.

Irvine, Delmar. *Writing About Music: A Style Book for Reports and Theses.* Seattle: University of Washington Press, 1956.

POSTSCRIPT

A Statement of Belief

One of man's basic needs is the desire for beauty. This desire can be satisfied through the aural, oral, or visual senses. Man satisfies this desire through these senses by actually creating the experience or by vicariously creating the experience. Music, appealing directly to the aural sense, is experienced through creating (composing) music or through re-creating (performing) music. It is vicariously experienced by the act of "listening." The depth and extent of these experiences depend on the ability to apprehend, and then to comprehend, that which makes the impact upon the aural sense. The more subtle the act of apprehension and comprehension, the more nearly perfect, or satisfying, is the fulfillment of the need for beauty.

Much of what is experienced in life is apprehended and comprehended without the need for formal tuition. Needless to say, these experiences fall in the realm of gross experiences. Such experiences often are called habits, customs, folkways and enable man to function minimally. The refinement of man's reactions to his experiences makes possible a more perfect life, a more satisfying life, a more rewarding life, a more efficient life. In our society this refinement is accomplished in a formal way — in "school." It is the duty of those charged with this refinement process to indicate, to develop, and to perfect the facts, skills, techniques, and aptitudes involved in the apprehending and comprehending of experiences.

In order to indicate, to develop, and to perfect the facts, skills, techniques, and aptitudes involved in the apprehending and comprehending of experiences one must, of course, have mastered them himself. He must be a highly "experienced" person — that is, he must bring to the refinement process a wealth of actual, real experience and an even greater wealth of vicarious experience. Second, he must possess the ability to order these experiences in a logical and sequential pattern so that reactions to further experiences will contribute to a more perfect, satisfying, rewarding, and efficient life. Third, that person charged with the refining process must possess the ability to communicate the facts, skills, techniques, and aptitudes to the student in a most efficient manner.

Society — our society in particular — has the responsibility of appointing only those people to the formal institutions established for refining man's reactions to his experiences who are "experienced," who can put in order, who can communicate. It then follows that the representatives of society in the appointive position must have earned that right because of their past "experienced" life, because of their skill in the logical and sequential ordering of experiences, and because of their proficiency in communication. In short, these representatives must truly be "refined." If society, and its representatives, assumes its responsibilities, then man's basic needs, of which the need for beauty is one, will be satisfied in more than a minimal manner. The extent beyond which man's basic needs are met minimally is a measure of society's culture, strength, and stability.

Bibliography

ALLEN, WILLIAM DWIGHT. *Philosophies of Music History.* New York: Dover Publications, Inc., 1962.

ARISTOTLE. *Politics,* translated by H. Rackham, The Loeb Classical Library. Cambridge: Harvard University Press, 1935.

BARR, A. S. "The Measurement and Prediction of Teaching Efficiency: A Summary of Investigations." *Journal of Experimental Education,* Vol. XVI (June, 1948).

————. "The Measurement of Teacher Characteristics and Prediction of Teacher Efficiency." *Review of Educational Research,* Vol. XXII (June, 1952).

————. "Wisconsin Studies of the Measurement and Prediction of Teacher Effectiveness." *Journal of Experimental Education,* Vol. XXX (Sept., 1961).

BARRETT, ROGER L. *The Study of the General Nature of Ideational Perception: Music.* Unpublished doctoral dissertation, University of Iowa, 1961. (*Dissertation Abstracts,* XXII/8/2814.)

BEAN, L. K. "An Experimental Approach to the Reading of Music." *Psychological Monographs,* Vol. 50, No. 6 (1938).

BERELSON, BERNARD and GARY E. STEINER. *Human Behavior: An Inventory of Scientific Findings.* New York: Harcourt, Brace, and World, Inc., 1964.

BIRCH, THOMAS E. *Musical Taste as Indicated by Records Owned by College Students with Varying High School Experiences.* Unpublished doctoral dissertation, University of Missouri, 1962. (*Dissertation Abstracts,* XIII/7/2545.)

BOARDMAN, EUNICE L. *An Investigation of the Effect of Preschool Training on the Development of Vocal Accuracy in Young Children.* Unpublished doctoral dissertation, University of Illinois, 1964. (*Dissertation Abstracts,* XXV/2/1245.)

BRITTON, ALLEN P. "Music in Early American Public Education: A Historical Critique." *Basic Concepts in Music Education,* The Fifty-seventh Yearbook of the National Society for the Study of Education, Part I. Chicago: University of Chicago Press, 1958.

BRUNER, JEROME S. *The Process of Education.* Cambridge: Harvard University Press, 1965.

————. *Toward a Theory of Instruction.* Cambridge: The Belknap Press of Harvard University Press, 1966.

BUTTS, R. FREEMAN and LAWRENCE A. CREMIN. *A History of Education in American Culture.* New York: Henry Holt and Co., 1953.

CHARTERS, W. W., JR. "Survival in the Profession: A Criterion for Selecting Teacher Trainees." *Journal of Teacher Education,* Vol. VII (Sept., 1956).

CHILDS, CARROLL A. *A Comparison of Two Distributed Instructional Periods in the Teaching of Beginning Instrumental Music Students.* Unpublished doctoral dissertation, Colorado State College, 1963. (*Dissertation Abstracts,* XX/1/517.)

COLEMAN, SATIS N. *Creative Music for Children.* New York: G. P. Putnam's Sons, 1928.

COMENIUS, JOHANN. *The Great Didactic,* translated by M. W. Keatinge. London: Adam and Charles Black, 1907.

CONANT, JAMES B. *The Education of American Teachers.* New York: McGraw-Hill Book Co., Inc., 1963.

COOK, E. T. and ALEXANDER WEDDERBURN, editors. *The Works of John Ruskin.* New York: Longmans, Green and Co., 1905.

DEWEY, JOHN. *How We Think.* Boston: D. C. Heath and Co., 1933.

————. *The School and Society.* Chicago: University of Chicago Press, 1902.

DOMAS, SIMEON J. and DAVID J. TIEDEMAN. "Teacher Competence: An Annotated Bibliography." *Journal of Experimental Education,* Vol. XIX (Dec., 1950).

DOWNEY, JUNE E. "A Musical Experiment." *American Journal of Psychology,* Vol. IX (1897).

EDSON, WILLIAM H. and CHARLES J. GLATZBACK. "Recruitment and Selective Admission of the Prospective Teacher." *Guidance in Teacher Education,* 37th Yearbook. The Association for Student Teaching, 1957.

ELLIS, HOWARD E. "Lowell Mason and the *Manual of the Boston Academy of Music.*" *Journal of Research in Music Education,* Vol. III (Spring, 1955).

————. *The Influence of Pestalozzianism on Instruction in Music.* Unpublished doctoral dissertation, University of Michigan, 1957.

FARNSWORTH, PAUL R. *The Social Psychology of Music.* New York: The Dryden Press, 1958.

FLAVELL, JOHN H. *The Developmental Psychology of Jean Piaget,* the University Series in Psychology, David C. McClelland, editor. Princeton: D. Van Nostrand Co., Inc., 1963.

FRANKLIN, E. *Tonality as a Basis for the Study of Musical Talent.* Gotëborg, Sweden: Gumperts Förlag, 1956.

FROEBEL, FRIEDRICH. *The Education of Man,* translated by W. N. Hailmann. New York: D. Appleton and Co., 1887.

GARDNER, JOHN W. "You Can Tell a Creative Company by the People it Keeps." *Think,* International Business Machines Corp., Vol. 28, No. 10 (Nov.-Dec., 1962).

GESLER, HARRIET L. *An Analysis of the Relation Between Pitch Discrimination and Phonic Sensitivity in First Grade Children.* Unpublished doctoral dissertation, University of Connecticut, 1958. (*Dissertation Abstracts,* XIX/5/988.)

GILMAN, BENJAMIN I. "Report on an Experimental Test of Musical Expressiveness." *American Journal of Psychology*, Vol. IV (1892).

GOOD, CARTER V. *and* DOUGLAS E. SCATES. *Methods of Research.* New York: Appleton-Century-Crofts, Inc., 1954.

GORDON, EDWIN. *Manual: Musical Aptitude Profile.* Boston: Houghton Mifflin Co., 1965.

GORDON, J. J. "How to Get Your Imagination Off the Ground." *Think*, International Business Machines Corp., Vol. 29, No. 3 (March, 1963).

GREEN, J. A., editor. *Pestalozzi's Educational Writings.* New York: Longmans, Green and Co., 1912.

GREULICH, W. W. and S. I. PYLE. *Radiographic Atlas of Skeletal Development of the Hand and Wrist*, 2nd ed. Palo Alto: Stanford University Press, 1959.

GUNDLACH, RALPH. "Factors Determining the Characterization of Musical Phrases." *American Journal of Psychology*, Vol. XLVII (1935).

HADOW, W. H. *Collected Essays.* London: Oxford University Press, 1928.

HALVERSON, H. M. *An Experimental Study of Prehension in Infants.* Genetic Psychology Monographs, Vol. X, No. 2 and 3 (1931).

HEINLEIN, C. P. "The Affective Character of the Major and Minor Modes in Music." *Journal of Comparative Psychology*, Vol. VIII (1928).

HELMHOLTZ, H. L. *On the Sensations of Tone as a Physiological Basis for the Theory of Music*, 4th ed. New York: Longmans, Green, Inc., 1912.

HEVNER, KATE. "The Affective Character of the Major and Minor Modes in Music." *American Journal of Psychology*, Vol. XLVII (1935).

——————. "The Affective Value of Pitch and Tempo in Music." *American Journal of Psychology*, Vol. XLIX (1937).

HIGHET, GILBERT. *The Art of Teaching.* New York: Vintage Books, 1959.

HUTTON, DORIS. "A Comparative Study of Two Methods of Training Sight-Singing in the Fourth Grade." *Journal of Research in Music Education*, Vol. 1 (1953).

JACKSON, PHILIP W. and JACOB W. GETZELS. *Creativity and Intelligence.* New York: Wiley, 1962.

JACOBSEN, O. I. "An Analytic Study of Eye-Movements in Reading Vocal and Instrumental Music." *Journal of Musicology*, Vol. 3 (1941).

JAQUES-DALCROZE, E. *Eurhythmics, Art, and Education*, translated by Frederick Rothwell, Cynthia Cox, editor. New York: A. S. Barnes & Co., 1930.

JOHN, ROBERT W. "Elam Ives and the Pestalozzian Philosophy of Education." *Journal of Research in Music Education*, Vol. VIII (Spring, 1960).

JONES, THERESA D. *The Development of Certain Motor Skills and Play Activities in Young Children.* Child Development Monographs, No. 26 (1939).

KAPLAN, MAX. *Foundations and Frontiers of Music Education.* New York: Holt, Rinehart and Winston, Inc., 1966.

KING, HARRY A. "A Study of the Relationship of Music Reading and I. Q. Scores." *Journal of Research in Music Education*, Vol. II, No. 1 (Spring, 1954).

——————. "Auditory and Visual Characteristics of Poor Music Readers." *Music Educators National Conference Yearbook*, 1939-40.

KODALY, ZOLTAN. *Choral Method*, adapted by Percy M. Young. New York: Boosey & Hawkes Music Publishers, Ltd., 1964.

KRESTEFF, ASSAN D. "The Growth of Musical Awareness in Children." *Bulletin* No. 1 (1963), Council for Research in Music Education.

KWALWASSER, JACOB. "Music Ability." *Music Education*, The Thirty-fifth Yearbook of the National Society for the Study of Education, Part II. Bloomington, Ill.: Public School Publishing Co., 1936.

KYME, GEORGE H. "Are Musical Tastes Indicative of Musical Capacity?" *Journal of Research in Music Education*, Vol. IV, No. 1 (Spring, 1956).

LANNERT, V. and M. ULLMAN. "Factors in the Reading of Piano Music." *American Journal of Psychology*, Vol. 58 (1945).

LEONHARD, CHARLES. "Newer Concepts in Learning Theory as They Apply to Music Education." *Bulletin* No. 1 (1963), Council for Research in Music Education.

LEUPOLD, ULRICH S., editor. *Liturgy and Hymns*, Vol. 53 of *Luther's Works*, Helmet T. Lehman, editor. Philadelphia: Fortress Press, 1965.

LOCKE, JOHN. *Some Thoughts Concerning Education*, R. H. Quick, editor. Cambridge: University Press, 1902.

MANN, HORACE. "Vocal Music." *Eighth Annual Report of the Board of Education, together with the Annual Report of the Secretary of the Board*. Boston: Dutton and Wentworth, 1845.

MANN, MARGARET. *Introduction to Cataloging and the Classification of Books*. Chicago: American Library Association, 1930.

McCARTHY, DOROTHEA. "Language Development." *Manual of Child Psychology*, Leonard Carmichael, editor. New York: Wiley, 1946.

McGRAW, M. S. *Growth: A Study of Johnny and Jimmy*. New York: D. Appleton-Century Co., 1935.

NEVINS, ALLEN. *The Gateway to History*. Boston: D. C. Heath and Co., 1938.

ODENWELLER, ARTHUR LEONARD. "Predicting the Quality of Teaching Success." *Teachers College Contributions to Education*, No. 676. New York: Bureau of Publications, Teachers College, Columbia University, 1936.

ORTMANN, O. "Span of Vision in Note Reading." *Journal*, Music Educators National Conference, Vol. 23 (1937).

————. "The Elements of Chord Reading in Music Notation." *Journal of Experimental Education*, Vol. 3 (1934).

————. "Tonal Intensity as an Aesthetic Factor." *Musical Quarterly*, Vol. XIV (1928).

PERNECKY, JACK M. "Action Research Methodology." *Bulletin* No. 1 (1963), Council for Research in Music Education.

PFLEDERER, MARILYN. "How Children Conceptually Organize Musical Sounds." *Bulletin* No. 7 (Spring, 1966), Council for Research in Music Education.

————. *The Responses of Children to Musical Tasks Embodying Piaget's Principle of Conservation*. Unpublished doctoral dissertation, University of Illinois, 1963. (*Dissertation Abstracts*, XXIV/11/4730.)

PIAGET, JEAN. *The Origins of Intelligence in Children*, translated by Margaret Cook. New York: International Universities Press, Inc., 1952.

———— and BÄRBEL INHELDER. *The Growth of Logical Thinking from Childhood to Adolescence*, translated by Anne Parsons and Stanley Milgram. New York: Basic Books, Inc., 1958.

Physical Growth. The Philadelphia Center for Research in Child Growth, n. d.

PLATO. *The Republic*, translated by Paul Shorey, The Loeb Classical Library. Cambridge: Harvard University Press, 1930-35.

REAM, M. J. *The Tapping Test — A Measure of Motility*. University of Iowa Studies in Psychology, Vol. VIII (1922).

RICHARDS, MARY HELEN. *Threshold to Music Program.* Palo Alto: Fearon Publishers, Inc., 1966.

RIGG, MELVIN. "An Experiment to Determine How Accurately College Students Can Interpret the Intended Meanings of Musical Compositions." *Journal of Experimental Psychology,* Vol. XXI (1937).

ROSS, VERNE RALPH. *Relationships Between Intelligence and Scholastic Achievement and Musical Talent.* Claremont, Calif.: California Bureau of Juvenile Research, 1937.

ROTHNEY, J. W. M. "Recent Findings in the Study of the Physical Growth of Children." *Journal of Educational Research,* Vol. XXXV, No. 3 (1941).

ROWEN, HELEN. "How to Produce an Idea." *Think,* International Business Machines Corp., Vol. 28, No. 10 (Nov.-Dec., 1962).

————. "The Creative People: How to Spot Them." *Think,* International Business Machines Corp., Vol. 28, No. 10 (Nov.-Dec., 1962).

RYANS, DAVID G. "Prediction of Teacher Effectiveness." *Encyclopedia of Educational Research,* Chester W. Harris, editor. New York: The Macmillan Co., 1960.

SCHOEN, MAX. *The Effects of Music.* New York: Harcourt, Brace, and Co., Inc., 1927.

SEASHORE, CARL E. *Psychology of Music.* New York: McGraw-Hill Book Co., Inc., 1938.

————. "The Discovery and Guidance of Musical Talent." *Educational Diagnosis,* The Thirty-fourth Yearbook of the National Society for the Study of Education. Bloomington, Ill.: Public School Publishing Co., 1935.

SHIRLEY, M. M. *The First Two Years.* Minneapolis: University of Minnesota Press, 1933.

SPENCER, HERBERT. *Education: Intellectual, Moral, and Physical.* New York: D. Appleton and Co., 1861.

ST. AUGUSTINE. *Confessions,* translated by William Watts, The Loeb Classical Library. New York: G. P. Putnam's Sons, 1912.

STANTON, HAZEL M. *Measurement of Musical Talent.* University of Iowa Studies in the Psychology of Music, Vol. II (1935).

STOUT, RUTH A. "Admissions and Retention Practices in College Programs of Teacher Education." *Personnel and Guidance Journal,* Vol. XXXIV (Dec., 1955).

STRANG, RUTH. *An Introduction to Child Study,* 4th ed. New York: The Macmillan Co., 1959.

TERMAN, LEWIS M. *Mental and Physical Traits of a Thousand Gifted Children,* Vol. I of *Genetic Studies of Genius.* Palo Alto: Stanford University Press, 1925.

VALENTINE, C. W. "The Aesthetic Appreciation of Musical Intervals Among School Children and Adults." *British Journal of Psychology,* Vol. VI (1913).

WALTER, ARNOLD. "Introduction." *Music for Children,* adapted by Doreen Hall and Arnold Walter. New York: Associated Music Publishers, Inc., 1955.

WEBER, MAX. *The Rational and Social Foundations of Music.* Munich, 1921. (Reprint by Southern Illinois University Press, Carbondale, Illinois, 1958.)

WELD, H. P. "An Experimental Study of Musical Enjoyment." *American Journal of Phychology,* Vol. XXIII (1912).

Index